New and Old Wars

New and Old Wars

Organized Violence in a Global Era

With an Afterword, January 2001

Mary Kaldor

Polity

First published in 1999 by Polity Press
in association with Blackwell Publishers Ltd
Reprinted in 1999
Reprinted with a new afterword 2001
Reprinted 2002
Editorial office:
Polity Press
65 Bridge Street
Cambridge CB2 1UR, UK

Marketing and production:
Blackwell Publishers Ltd
108 Cowley Road
Oxford OX4 1JF, UK

ISBN 0–7456–2066–3
ISBN 0–7456–2067–1 (pbk)

A catalogue record for this book is available from the British Library.

Typeset in 11 on 13 pt Berling
by Ace Filmsetting Ltd, Frome, Somerset
Printed in Great Britain by T. J. International, Padstow, Cornwall

This book is printed on acid-free paper.

Contents

Acknowledgements

I am very grateful to a number of people who read the manuscript and gave me valuable comments and I should like to thank, particularly, Ulrich Albrecht, Mient Jan Faber, Zdenek Kavan, Julian Perry Robinson, Martin Shaw and the anonymous reader at Polity Press. Needless to say, they are not responsible for the final result. I should also like to thank Aimée Shalan for help with the manuscript and everyone at Polity, especially David Held, for support and encouragement.

Parts of chapter 3 were incorporated into a chapter written jointly by me and Vesna Bojičić, 'The Political Economy of War in Bosnia–Herzegovina', in Mary Kaldor and Basker Vashee (eds), *Restructuring the Global Military Sector: New Wars* (Cassell/Pinter, 1997). An earlier version of chapter 4 was published as 'Cosmopolitanism versus nationalism: the new divide?', in Richard Caplan and John Feffer (eds), *Europe's New Nationalisms* (Cambridge University Press, 1996).

Abbreviations

ABiH	Army of Bosnia–Herzegovina
ANC	African National Congress
BRA	Bourgainville Revolutionary Army
BSA	Bosnian Serb Army
CIS	Commonwealth of Independent States
ECHO	European Community Humanitarian Office
ECOMOG	Economic Community of West African States Ceasefire Monitoring Group
ECOWAS	Economic Community of West African States
EU	European Union
GDP	Gross Domestic Product
HCA	Helsinki Citizens' Assembly
HDZ	Croatian Democratic Party
HOS	Paramilitary wing of HSP
HSP	Croatian Party of Rights
HV	Croatian Army
HVO	Croatian Defence Council
ICC	International Criminal Court
ICFY	International Conference on Former Yugoslavia
ICRC	International Committee of the Red Cross
IDP	Internally displaced person
IFOR	Implementation Force
IFP	Inkatha Freedom Party
IISS	International Institute for Strategic Studies
IMF	International Monetary Fund

IRA	Irish Republican Army
JNA	Yugoslav National Army
MOS	Muslim Armed Forces
MPRI	Military Professional Resources Incorporated
NACC	NATO Coordination Council
NATO	North Atlantic Treaty Organization
NGO	Non-governmental organization
OAU	Organization of African Unity
OSCE	Organization for Security and Cooperation in Europe
PASOK	Panhellenic Socialist Movement (Greece)
RENAMO	Resistência Nacional Mocambiçana
SCR	Security Council Resolution
SDA	(Muslim) Party of Democratic Action
SDS	Serbian Democratic Party
SFOR	Stabilization Force
SPLA	Sudan People's Liberation Army
TO	Territorial Defence Units
UN	United Nations
UNHCR	United Nations High Commissioner for Refugees
UNICEF	United Nations Children's Fund
UNPROFOR	United Nations Protection Force
UNU	United Nations University
WEU	Western European Union
WIDER	World Institute for Development Economics Research

1

Introduction

In the summer of 1992, I visited Nagorno-Karabakh in the Transcaucasian region in the midst of a war involving Azerbaijan and Armenia. It was then that I realized that what I had previously observed in the former Yugoslavia was not unique; it was not a throwback to the Balkan past but rather a contemporary predicament especially, or so I thought, to be found in the post-communist part of the world. The wild west atmosphere of Knin (then the capital of the self-proclaimed Serbian republic in Croatia) and Nagorno-Karabakh, peopled by young men in home-made uniforms, desperate refugees and thuggish, neophyte politicians, was quite distinctive. Later, I embarked on a research project on the character of the new type of wars and I discovered from my colleagues who had first-hand experience of Africa that what I had noted in Eastern Europe shared many common features with the wars taking place in Africa and perhaps also other places, for example South Asia. Indeed, the experience of wars in other places shed new light on my understanding of what was happening in the Balkans and the former Soviet Union.[1]

My central argument is that, during the 1980s and 1990s, a new type of organized violence has developed, especially in Africa and Eastern Europe, which is one aspect of the current globalized era. I describe this type of violence as 'new war'. I use the term 'new' to distinguish these wars from prevailing perceptions of war drawn from an earlier era, which I outline in chapter 2. I use the term 'war' to emphasize the political nature of this new type of violence, even though, as will become clear in the following pages, the new wars involve a blurring of the distinctions between war (usually defined as violence between states or organized political groups for political motives), organized crime (violence undertaken by privately organized groups for private purposes, usually financial gain) and large-scale violations of human rights (violence undertaken by states or politically organized groups against individuals).

In most of the literature, the new wars are described as internal or civil wars or else as 'low-intensity conflict'. Yet although most of these wars are localized, they involve a myriad of transnational connections so that the distinction between internal and external, between aggression (attacks from abroad) and repression (attacks from inside the country), or even between local and global, are difficult to sustain. The term 'low-intensity conflict' was coined during the Cold War period by the US military to describe guerrilla warfare or terrorism. Although it is possible to trace the evolution of the new wars from the so-called low-intensity conflicts of the Cold War period, they have distinctive characteristics which are masked by what is in effect a catch-all term. Some authors describe the new wars as privatized or informal wars;[2] yet, while the privatization of violence is an important element of these wars, in practice, the distinction between what is private and what is public, state and non-state, informal and formal, between what is done for economic or political motives, cannot easily be applied. A more appropriate term is perhaps the term 'post-modern', which is used by several authors.[3] Like 'new wars', it offers a way of distinguishing these wars from the wars which could be said to be characteristic of classical modernity. However, the term is also used to refer to virtual wars and wars in cyberspace;[4] moreover, the new wars involve elements of pre-modernity and modernity as well. Finally, Martin Shaw uses the term 'degenerate warfare'. For him there is a continuity with the total wars of the twentieth century and their genocidal aspects; the term draws attention to the decay of the national frameworks, especially military forces.[5]

Among American strategic writers, there is a discussion about what is known as the Revolution in Military Affairs.[6] The argument is that the advent of information technology is as significant as was the advent of the tank and the aeroplane, or even as significant as the shift from horsepower to mechanical power, with profound implications for the future of warfare. However, the Revolution in Military Affairs is conceived by these writers within the inherited institutional structures of war and the military. They envisage wars on a traditional model in which the new techniques develop in a more or less linear extension from the past. Moreover, they are designed to sustain the imagined character of war which was typical of the Cold War era and utilized in such a way as to minimize own casualties. The preferred technique is spectacular aerial bombing which reproduces the appearance of classical war for public consumption and which has very little to do with reality on the ground. Hence Baudrillard's famous remark that the Gulf War did not take place.[7] These complex sophisticated techniques have been used not only in Iraq, but also in Bosnia–Herzegovina and Somalia with, I would argue, relatively little practical relevance even though they have caused many civilian casualties.

I share the view that there has been a revolution in military affairs, but it is a revolution in the social relations of warfare, not in technology, even though the changes in social relations are influenced by and make use of new technology. Beneath the spectacular displays are real wars, which, even in the case of the 1991 Iraq war in which hundreds and thousands of Kurds and Shiites died, are better explained in terms of my conception of new wars.

I argue that the new wars have to be understood in the context of the process known as globalization. By globalization, I mean the intensification of global interconnectedness – political, economic, military and cultural. Even though I accept the argument that globalization has its roots in modernity or even earlier, I consider that the globalization of the 1980s and 1990s is a qualitatively new phenomenon which can, at least in part, be explained as a consequence of the revolution in information technologies and dramatic improvements in communication and data-processing. This process of intensifying interconnectedness is a contradictory process involving both integration and fragmentation, homogenization and diversification, globalization and localization. It is often argued that the new wars are a consequence of the end of the Cold War; they reflect a power vacuum which is typical of transition periods in world affairs. It is undoubtedly true that the consequences of the end of the Cold

War – the availability of surplus arms, the discrediting of socialist ideologies, the disintegration of totalitarian empires, the withdrawal of superpower support to client regimes – contributed in
important ways to the new wars. But equally, the end of the
Cold War could be viewed as the way in which the Eastern bloc
succumbed to the inevitable encroachment of globalization –
the crumbling of the last bastions of territorial autarchy, the
moment when Eastern Europe was 'opened up' to the rest of
the world.

The impact of globalization is visible in many of the new wars.
The global presence in these wars can include international re-
porters, mercenary troops and military advisers, diaspora volunteers as well as a veritable 'army' of international agencies ranging
from non-governmental organizations (NGOs) like Oxfam, Save
the Children, Médecins Sans Frontières, Human Rights Watch
and the International Red Cross to international institutions like
the United Nations High Commissioner for Refugees (UNHCR),
the European Union (EU), the United Nations Children's Fund
(UNICEF), the Organization for Security and Cooperation in
Europe (OSCE), the Organization for African Unity (OAU) and
the United Nations (UN) itself, including peacekeeping troops.
Indeed, the wars epitomize a new kind of global/local divide
between those members of a global class who can speak English,
have access to faxes, e-mail and satellite television, who use dollars or deutschmarks or credit cards, and who can travel freely,
and those who are excluded from global processes, who live off
what they can sell or barter or what they receive in humanitarian aid, whose movement is restricted by roadblocks, visas and
the cost of travel, and who are prey to sieges, forced famines,
landmines, etc.

In the literature on globalization, a central concern has to do
with the implications of global interconnectedness for the future of the territorially based sovereignty – that is to say, for the
future of the modern state.[8] The new wars arise in the context
of the erosion of the autonomy of the state and in some extreme
cases the disintegration of the state. In particular, they occur in
the context of the erosion of the monopoly of legitimate organized violence. This monopoly is eroded from above and from
below. It has been eroded from above by the transnationalization
of military forces which began during the two world wars and
was institutionalized by the bloc system during the Cold War

and by innumerable transnational connections between armed forces that developed in the post-war period.[9] The capacity of states to use force unilaterally against other states has been greatly weakened. This is partly for practical reasons – the growing destructiveness of military technology and the increasing interconnectedness of states, especially in the military field. It is difficult to imagine nowadays a state or group of states risking a large-scale war which could be even more destructive than what was experienced during the first and second world wars. Moreover, military alliances, international arms production and trade, various forms of military cooperation and exchanges, arms control agreements, etc. have created a form of global military integration. It is also due to the evolution of international norms. The principle that unilateral aggression is illegitimate was first codified in the Kellogg–Briand pact of 1928, and reinforced after World War II in the UN Charter and through the reasoning used in the war crimes trials in Nuremberg and Tokyo.

At the same time, the monopoly of organized violence is eroded from below by privatization. Indeed, it could be argued that the new wars are part of a process which is more or less a reversal of the processes through which modern states evolved. As I argue in chapter 2, the rise of the modern state was intimately connected to war. In order to fight wars, rulers needed to increase taxation and borrowing, to eliminate 'wastage' as a result of crime, corruption and inefficiency, to regularize armed forces and police and to eliminate private armies, and to mobilize popular support in order to raise money and men. As war became the exclusive province of the state, so the growing destructiveness of war against other states was paralleled by a process of growing security at home; hence the way in which the term 'civil' came to mean internal. The new wars occur in situations in which state revenues decline because of the decline of the economy as well as the spread of criminality, corruption and inefficiency, violence is increasingly privatized both as a result of growing organized crime and the emergence of paramilitary groups, and political legitimacy is disappearing. Thus the distinctions between external barbarity and domestic civility, between the combatant as the legitimate bearer of arms and the non-combatant, between the soldier or policeman and the criminal, are breaking down. The barbarity of war between states may have become a thing of the past. In its place is a new type of organized violence that is more pervasive, but also perhaps less extreme.

In chapter 3, I use the example of the war in Bosnia–Herzegovina to illustrate the main features of the new wars, mainly because it is the war with which I am most familiar. The war in Bosnia–Herzegovina shares many of the characteristics of wars in other places. But in one sense it is exceptional; it has become the focus of global attention. More resources – governmental and non-governmental – have been concentrated there than in any other new war. On the one hand, this means that, as a case study, it has atypical features. On the other hand, it also means that it has become the paradigm case, from which different lessons are drawn, the example which is used to argue out different general positions, and, at the same time, a laboratory in which different ways of managing the new wars are experimented.

The new wars can be contrasted with earlier wars in terms of their goals, the methods of warfare and how they are financed. The goals of the new wars are about identity politics in contrast to the geo-political or ideological goals of earlier wars. In chapter 4, I argue that, in the context of globalization, ideological and/or territorial cleavages of an earlier era have increasingly been supplanted by an emerging political cleavage between what I call cosmopolitanism, based on inclusive, universalist, multicultural values, and the politics of particularist identities.[10] This cleavage can be explained in terms of the growing divide between those who are part of global processes and those who are excluded, but it should not be equated with this division. Among the global class are members of transnational networks based on exclusivist identity, while at the local level there are many courageous individuals who refuse the politics of particularism.

By identity politics, I mean the claim to power on the basis of a particular identity – be it national, clan, religious or linguistic. In one sense, all wars involve a clash of identities – British against French, communists against democrats. But my point is that these earlier identities were either linked to a notion of state interest or to some forward-looking project – ideas about how society should be organized. Nineteenth-century European nationalisms or post-colonial nationalisms, for example, presented themselves as emancipatory nation-building projects. The new identity politics is about the claim to power on the basis of labels – in so far as there are ideas about political or social change, they tend to relate to an idealized nostalgic representation of the past. It is often claimed that the new wave of identity politics is merely a throwback to the past, a resurgence of ancient hatreds kept under control by colonialism and/or the Cold War. While it is true that the narratives of identity politics depend on memory and tradition, it is also the case that these are 'reinvented' in the context of the failure or the corrosion of other sources of political legitimacy – the discrediting of socialism or the nation-building rhetoric of the first generation of post-colonial leaders. These backward-looking political projects arise in the vacuum created by the absence of forward-looking projects. Unlike the politics of ideas which are open to all and therefore tend to be integrative, this type of identity politics is inherently exclusive and therefore tends to fragmentation.

There are two aspects of the new wave of identity politics which specifically relate to the process of globalization. First, the new wave of identity politics is both local and global, national as well as transnational. In many cases, there are significant diaspora communities whose influence is greatly enhanced by the ease of travel and improved communication. Alienated diaspora groups in advanced industrial or oil-rich countries provide ideas, funds and techniques, thereby imposing their own frustrations and fantasies on what is often a very different situation. Second, this politics makes use of the new technology. The speed of political mobilization is greatly increased by the use of the electronic media. The effect of television, radio or videos on what is often a non-reading public cannot be overestimated. The protagonists of the new politics often display the symbols of a global mass culture – Mercedes cars, Rolex watches, Rayban sunglasses – combined with the labels that signify their own brand of particularistic cultural identity.

The second characteristic of the new wars is the changed mode of warfare[11] – the means through which the new wars are fought. The strategies of the new warfare draw on the experience of both guerrilla warfare and counterinsurgency, yet they are quite distinctive. In conventional or regular war, the goal is the capture of territory by military means; battles are the decisive encounters of the war. Guerrilla warfare developed as a way of getting round the massive concentrations of military force which are characteristic of conventional war. In guerrilla warfare, territory is captured through political control of the population rather than through military advance, and battles are avoided as far as possible. The new warfare also tends to avoid battle and to control territory through political control of the population, but whereas guerrilla warfare, at least in theory as articulated by Mao Tse-tung or Che Guevara, aimed to capture 'hearts and minds', the new warfare borrows from counterinsurgency techniques of destabilization aimed at sowing 'fear and hatred'. The aim is to control the population by getting rid of everyone of a different identity (and indeed of a different opinion). Hence the strategic goal of these wars is population expulsion through various means such as mass killing, forcible resettlement, as well as a range of political, psychological and economic techniques of intimidation. This is why, in all these wars, there has been a dramatic increase in the number of refugees and displaced persons, and why most violence is directed against civilians. At the turn of the century, the ratio of military to civilian casualties in wars was 8:1. Today, this has been almost exactly reversed; in the wars of the 1990s, the ratio of military to civilian casualties is approximately 1:8. Behaviour that was proscribed according to the classical rules of warfare and codified in the laws of war in the late nineteenth century and early twentieth century, such as atrocities against non-combatants, sieges, destruction of historic monuments, etc., now constitutes an essential component of the strategies of the new mode of warfare.

In contrast to the vertically organized hierarchical units that were typical of 'old wars', the units that fight these wars include a disparate range of different types of groups such as paramilitary units, local warlords, criminal gangs, police forces, mercenary groups and also regular armies including breakaway units of regular armies. In organizational terms, they are highly decentralized and they operate through a mixture of confrontation and co-operation even when on opposing sides. They make use of advanced technology even if it is not what we tend to call 'high technology' (stealth bombers or cruise missiles, for example). In the last fifty years, there have been significant advances in lighter weapons – undetectable landmines, for example, or small arms which are light, accurate and easy to use so that they can even be operated by children. They also make use of modern communications – cellular phones or computer links – in order to coordinate, mediate and negotiate among the disparate fighting units.

The third way in which the new wars can be contrasted with earlier wars is what I call the new 'globalized' war economy, which is elaborated in chapter 5 along with the mode of warfare. The new globalized war economy is almost exactly the opposite of the war economies of the two world wars. The latter were centralized, totalizing and autarchic. The new war economies are decentralized. Participation in the war is low and unemployment is extremely high. Moreover, these economies are heavily dependent on external resources. In these wars, domestic production declines dramatically because of global competition, physical destruction or interruptions to normal trade, as does tax revenue. In these circumstances, the fighting units finance themselves through plunder and the black market or through external assistance. The latter can take the following forms: remittances from the diaspora, 'taxation' of humanitarian assistance, support from neighbouring governments or illegal trade in arms, drugs or valuable commodities such as oil or diamonds. All of these sources can only be sustained through continued violence so that a war logic is built into the functioning of the economy. This retrograde set of social relationships, which is entrenched by war, has a tendency to spread across borders through refugees or organized crime or ethnic minorities. It is possible to identify clusters of war economies or near war economies in places like the Balkans, the Caucasus, Central Asia, the Horn of Africa, Central Africa or West Africa.

Because the various warring parties share the aim of sowing 'fear and hatred', they operate in a way that is mutually reinforcing, helping each other to create a climate of insecurity and suspicion – indeed, it is possible to find examples in both Eastern Europe and Africa of mutual cooperation for both military and economic purposes. Often, among the first civilians to be targeted are those who espouse a different politics, who try to maintain inclusive social relations and some sense of public morality. Thus though the new wars appear to be between different linguistic, religious or tribal groups, they can also be presented as wars in which those who represent particularistic identity politics cooperate in suppressing the values of civility and multiculturalism. In other words, they can be understood as wars between exclusivism and cosmopolitanism.

This analysis of new wars has implications for the management of conflicts, which I explore in chapter 6. There is no possible long-term solution within the framework of identity politics. And because these are conflicts with extensive social and economic ramifications, top-down approaches are likely to fail. In the early 1990s there was great optimism about the prospects for humanitarian intervention to protect civilians. However, the practice of humanitarian intervention has, I would argue, been shackled by a kind of myopia about the character of the new warfare. The persistence of inherited mandates, the tendency to interpret these wars in traditional terms, has been the main reason why humanitarian intervention has not only failed to prevent the wars but may have actually helped to sustain them in various ways, for example, through the provision of humanitarian aid, which is an important source of income for the warring parties, or through the legitimation of war criminals by inviting them to the negotiating table, or through the effort to find political compromises based on exclusivist assumptions.

The key to any long-term solution is the restoration of legitimacy, the reconstitution of the control of organized violence by public authorities, whether local, national or global. This is both a political process – the rebuilding of trust in and support for public authorities – and a legal process – the re-establishment of a rule of law within which public authorities operate. This cannot be done on the basis of particularistic politics. An alternative forward-looking cosmopolitan political project which would cross the global/local divide and reconstruct legitimacy around an inclusive, democratic set of values has to be counterposed against the politics of exclusivism. In all the new wars there are local people and places who struggle against the politics of exclusivism – the Hutus and Tutsis who called themselves Hutsis and tried to defend their localities against genocide, the non-nationalists in the cities of Bosnia–Herzegovina, particularly Sarajevo and Tuzla, who kept alive civic multicultural values, the elders in Northwest Somaliland who negotiated peace. What is needed is an alliance between local defenders of civility and transnational institutions which would guide a strategy aimed at controlling violence. Such a strategy would include political, military and economic components. It would operate within a framework of international law, based on that body of international law that comprises both the laws of warfare and human rights, which could perhaps be termed cosmopolitan law. In this context, peacekeeping could be reconceptualized as cosmopolitan law-enforcement. Since the new wars are, in a sense, a mixture of war, crime and human rights violations, so the agents of cosmopolitan law-enforcement have to be a mixture of soldiers and policemen. I also argue that a new strategy of reconstruction, which includes the reconstruction of social, civic and institutional relationships, should supplant the current dominant approaches of structural adjustment or humanitarianism.

In the final chapter of the book, I discuss the implications of the argument for global order. Although the new wars are concentrated in Africa, Eastern Europe and Asia, they are a global phenomenon not just because of the presence of global and global networks, nor because they are reported globally. The characteristics of the new wars I have described are to be found in North America and Western Europe as well. The right-wing militia groups in the United States are not so very different from the paramilitary groups in Eastern Europe or Africa. Indeed, in the United States it is reported that private security officers outnumber police officers by 2:1. Nor is the salience of identity politics and the growing disillusionment with formal politics just a Southern and Eastern phenomenon. The violence in the inner cities of Western Europe and North America can, in some senses, be described as new wars. It is sometimes said that the advanced industrial world is integrating and the poorer parts of the world are fragmenting. I would argue that all parts of the world are characterized by a combination of integration and fragmentation even though the tendencies to integration are greater in the North and the tendencies to fragmentation may be greater in the South and East.

It is no longer possible to insulate parts of the world from other parts. Neither the idea that we can re-create some kind of bipolar or multipolar world order on the basis of identity – Christianity versus Islam, for example – nor the idea that the 'anarchy' in places like Africa and Eastern Europe can be contained is feasible if my analysis of the changing character of organized violence has some basis in reality. This is why the cosmopolitan project has to be a global project even if it is, as it must be, local or regional in application.

The book is based, first and foremost, on direct experience of the new wars, especially in the Balkans and the Transcaucasian region. As one of the Chairs of the Helsinki Citizens' Assembly (HCA), I have travelled extensively in these areas and learned much of what I know from the critical intellectuals and activists involved in local branches of the HCA. In particular, in Bosnia–Herzegovina, HCA was given the status of an implementing agency of UNHCR, which enabled me to move around the country during the war in support of local activists. I was also lucky enough to have access to the various institutions responsible for carrying out the policies of the international community; as chair of HCA, it was one of my tasks, along with others, to present the ideas and proposals of local branches to governments and international institutions such as the EU, NATO, the OSCE and the UN. As an academic, I was able to supplement and put into context this knowledge through reading, through exchanges with colleagues working in related fields and through research projects undertaken for the United Nations University (UNU) and the European Commission.[12] In particular, I was greatly helped by the newsletters, news digests, pleas for help and monitoring reports that now can be received daily on the internet.

The aim of this book is not simply to inform, although I have tried to provide information and to back my assertions with examples. The aim is to offer a different perspective, the perspective derived from the experiences of critically minded individuals on the ground, tempered by my own experience in various international fora. It is a contribution to the reconceptualization of patterns of violence and war that has to be undertaken if the tragedies that are encroaching in many parts of the world are to be halted. I am not an optimist, yet my practical suggestions may seem utopian. I offer them in hope, not in confidence, as the only alternative to a grim future.

2
Old Wars

As Clausewitz was fond of pointing out, war is a social activity.[1] It involves the mobilization and organization of individual men, almost never women, for the purpose of inflicting physical violence; it entails the regulation of certain types of social relationships and has its own particular logic. Clausewitz, who was arguably the greatest exponent of modern war, insisted that war could not be reduced either to art or to science. Sometimes, he likened war to business competition and often used economic analogies to illustrate his points.

Every society has its own characteristic form of war. What we tend to perceive as war, what policy-makers and military leaders define as war, is, in fact, a specific phenomenon which took shape in Europe somewhere between the fifteenth and eighteenth centuries, although it has passed through several different phases since then. It was a phenomenon that was intimately bound up with the evolution of the modern state. It went through several phases, as I have tried to show in table 2.1, from the relatively limited wars of the seventeenth and eighteenth centuries associated with the growing power of the absolutist state, to the more revolutionary wars of the nineteenth century such as the Napoleonic Wars or the American Civil War, both of which were linked to the establishment of nation-states, to the total wars of the early twentieth century, and the imagined Cold War of the late twentieth century, which were wars of alliances and, later, blocs. Each of these phases was characterized by a different mode

Table 2.1 *The evolution of old wars*

	17th and 18th centuries	*19th century*	*Early 20th century*	*Late 20th century*
Type of polity	absolutist state	nation-state	coalitions of states; multinational states; empires	blocs
Goals of war	reasons of state; dynastic conflict; consolidation of borders	national conflict	national and ideological conflict	ideological conflict
Type of army	mercenary/professional	professional/conscription	mass armies	scientific-military elite/professional armies
Military technique	use of firearms, defensive manoeuvres, seiges	railways and telegraph, rapid mobilization	massive firepower; tanks and aircraft	nuclear weapons
War economy	regularization of taxation and borrowing	expansion of administration and bureaucracy	mobilization economy	military-industrial complex

of warfare, involving different types of military forces, different strategies and techniques, different relations and means of warfare. But despite these differences, war was recognizably the same phenomenon: a construction of the centralized, 'rationalized', hierarchically ordered, territorialized modern state. As the centralized, territorialized modern state gives way to new types of polity emerging out of new global processes, so war, as we presently conceive it, is becoming an anachronism.

This chapter aims to provide a stylized description of old wars. Actual warfare never exactly fitted the stylized description. This type of war was predominantly European. There were always rebellions, colonial wars or guerrilla wars, both in Europe and elsewhere. They were sometimes described as 'irregular warfare' or else not called war at all. Instead, they were called uprisings, insurgencies or, more recently, low-intensity conflict. Nevertheless, it is the stylized notion of war that still profoundly affects our thinking about war and dominates, even today, the way policy-makers conceive of security.

War and the Emergence of the Modern State

Clausewitz defined war as 'an act of violence intended to compel our opponent to fulfill our will'.[2] This definition implied that 'we' and 'our opponent' were states, and the 'will' of one state could be clearly defined. Hence war, in the Clausewitzean definition, is war between states for a definable political end, i.e. state interest.

The notion of war as state activity was only firmly established towards the end of the eighteenth century. The only precedent for this type of war was ancient Rome, although even in this case it was one-sided; the state, i.e. Rome, fought against barbarians who had no notion of the separation of state and society. Van Creveld argues that war between the Greek city-states did not count as state warfare since there was no clear distinction between the state and the citizens. Wars were fought by citizen militias, and contemporary accounts of warfare tended to refer to war between 'the Athenians' and 'the Spartans' rather than to war between 'Athens' and 'Sparta'.[3] Between the fall of the Roman Empire and the late Middle Ages, war was fought by a variety of actors – the Church, feudal barons, barbarian tribes,

city-states – each with its own characteristic military formations.
Hence, the barbarian mode of fighting was generally based on
warrior cults, the individual warrior being the key military unit.
Feudal barons depended on knights, with their codes of honour
and chivalry, supported by serfs. The city-states of Northern Italy
typically depended on citizen militias much like the earlier Greek
city-states.

In the early stages of European state formation, monarchs
raised armies to fight wars from coalitions of feudal barons rather
as the UN Secretary-General, today, has to mobilize voluntary
contributions from individual states in order to raise a peacekeeping force. Gradually, they were able to consolidate territorial borders and to centralize power by using their growing
economic power, derived from customs duties, various forms
of taxation and borrowing from the emergent bourgeoisie, to
raise mercenary armies which gave them a certain degree of
independence from the barons. However, mercenary armies
turned out to be unreliable; their loyalty could not be counted
on. Moreover, they were disbanded after wars or for the winter. The cost of disbandment and of re-enlistment was often
prohibitive and, in the closed seasons, the mercenaries could
always find other less acceptable ways of making a living. Thus,
mercenary armies came to be replaced by standing armies which
enabled monarchs to create specialized, professional military
forces. The introduction of drill and exercise, pioneered by
Gustav Adolphus of Sweden and Prince William of Orange,
kept the army occupied in periods when there was no open
warfare. According to Keegan, the establishment of permanent
infantry troops, the creation of *compagnies d'ordonnance* or regi-
ments became the 'device for securing the control of armed
force by the state'. They were kept in garrison towns which
became 'schools of the nation'.[4] Uniforms were introduced to
distinguish soldiers from civilians. As Michael Roberts puts it,
'the soldier became the King's man for he wore the King's coat'.[5]
Literally, as it turned out, because kings increasingly tended to
wear military uniforms to exhibit their roles as military commanders.

The new type of military organization was to become typical
of the emerging administrative arrangements that were associated with modernity. The soldier was the agent of what Max
Weber called rational-legal authority:

The modern military officer is a type of appointed official who is clearly marked out by certain class distinctions . . . In this respect, such officers differ radically from elected military leaders; from charismatic condottieri; from the type of officers who recruit and lead mercenary armies as a capitalistic enterprise; and finally from the incumbents of commissions which have been purchased. There may be gradual transitions between these types. The patrimonial 'retainer' who is separated from the means of carrying out his function and the proprietor of a mercenary army for capitalistic purposes, have along with the private capitalistic entrepreneur, become pioneers of the modern type of bureaucracy.[6]

The establishment of standing armies under the control of the state was an integral part of the monopolization of legitimate violence which was intrinsic to the modern state. State interest became the legitimate justification for war, supplanting concepts of justice, *jus ad bellum*, drawn from theology. The Clausewitzean insistence that war is a rational instrument for the pursuit of state interest – 'the continuation of politics by other means' – constituted a secularization of legitimacy that paralleled developments in other spheres of activity. Once state interest had become the dominant legitimation of war, then claims of just cause by non-state actors could no longer be pursued through violent means.

In the same vein, there developed rules about what constituted legitimate warfare which were later codified in the laws of war. All types of warfare are characterized by rules; the very fact that warfare is a socially sanctioned activity, that it has to be organized and justified, requires rules. There is a thin dividing line between socially acceptable killing and what is ostracized by society. But that dividing line is defined differently in different periods. In the Middle Ages, the rules of warfare, *jus in bello*, were derived from papal authority. Under the modern state, a new set of secular rules had to be evolved. According to van Creveld:

To distinguish war from mere crime, it was defined as something waged by sovereign states and by them alone. Soldiers were defined as personnel licensed to engage in armed violence on behalf of the state . . . To obtain and maintain their license, soldiers had to be carefully registered, marked and controlled to the exclusion of privateering. They were supposed to fight only when in uniform, carrying their arms 'openly' and obeying a commander who could be held responsible for their actions. They were not supposed to resort to 'dastardly' methods such as violating truces, taking up arms again after they had been taken prisoner, and the like. The civilian population was supposed to be left alone, 'military necessity' permitting.[7]

In order to finance standing armies, administration, taxation and borrowing had to be regularized. Throughout the eighteenth century, military spending accounted for around three-quarters of state budgets in most European states. Administrative reform had to be undertaken to improve tax-raising capacities; corruption had to be limited, if not eliminated, to prevent 'leakage'.[8] War offices and secretaries of war had to be established to organize and improve the efficiency of expenditure. To extend borrowing, it was necessary to regularize the banking system and the creation of money, to separate the king's finance from the finance of the state and, ultimately, to establish central banks.[9]

Likewise, other means had to be found to establish law and order and justice within the territory of the state both to provide a secure basis for taxation and borrowing and for legitimacy. A kind of implicit contract was established whereby kings offered protection in exchange for funds. The elimination and/or outlawing of brigands, privateers and highwaymen eliminated private forms of 'protection', thus swelling the king's revenue-raising capacity, and created a basis for legitimate economic activity. Hence, parallel to the redefinition of war as war between states, as an external activity, was the process Anthony Giddens calls internal pacification, which included the introduction of monetary relations – e.g. wages and rent – in place of more direct coercion, the phasing out of violent forms of punishment such as flogging and hanging, and the establishment of civilian agencies for tax collection and domestic law-enforcement. Particularly important was the emerging distinction between the military and the civilian police responsible for domestic law and order.[10]

The process of monopolization of violence was by no means smooth and uninterrupted, nor did it take place at the same time or in the same way in different European states. The Prussian state, created after the Treaty of Westphalia out of the various pieces of territory held by the House of Hohenzollern, is often considered a model. This state, which was an entirely artificial creation, was able in the eighteenth century to match the military strength of France with only one-fifth of the population, owing to the vigorous combination of military reform and rational administration introduced by Frederick William, the Great Elector, and his successors. In contrast, French kings faced continuous rebellions by the nobility and had enormous difficulty in regularizing administration and tax collection. Skocpol argues that a central consideration in explaining the French Revolution was the inability of the *ancien régime* to develop the administrative and financial capacity necessary to realize its military ambitions.[11]

Nor was the process as rational or as functional as this stylized description suggests. Michael Roberts insisted that it was military logic that led to the formation of standing armies. But it is difficult to distinguish the exigencies of war from the demands of domestic consolidation. Cardinal Richelieu favoured the establishment of a standing army because he saw it as a way to bring the nobles under control. Rousseau consistently argued that war was directed as much against subjects as against other states:

> Again, anyone can understand that war and conquest without and the encroachments of despotism within give each other mutual support; that money and men are habitually taken at pleasure from a people of slaves to bring others beneath the same yoke; and that conversely war furnishes a pretext for exactions of money and another, no less plausible, for keeping large armies constantly on foot, to hold people at awe. In a word, anyone can see that aggressive princes wage war at least as much on their subjects as on their enemies, and that the conquering nation is left no better off than the conquered.[12]

While rational state interest was claimed to be the goal of war, more emotive causes have always been required to instil loyalty and to persuade men to risk their lives. It was, after all, religious fervour that inspired Cromwell's New Model Army, which was the earliest example of a modern professional force. Prussian success is often attributed to the force of Lutheranism.

By the end of the eighteenth century, it was possible to define the specific socially organized activity which we perceive as war.

It could be situated in the context of a whole series of new distinctions which were characteristic of the evolving state. These included:

- the distinction between public and private, between the sphere of state activity and non-state activity;
- the distinction between internal and external, between what took place within the clearly defined territory of the state and what took place outside;
- the distinction between the economic and the political which was associated with the rise of capitalism, the separation of private economic activity from public state activities, and the removal of physical coercion from economic activities;
- the distinction between the civil and the military, between domestic non-violent legal intercourse and external violent struggle, between civil society and barbarism;
- the distinction between the legitimate bearer of arms and the non-combatant or the criminal.

Above all, there emerged the distinction between war and peace itself. In place of more or less continuous violent activity, war became a discrete event, an aberration in what appeared to be a progressive evolution towards a civil society, not in today's sense of active citizenry and organized NGOs, but in the sense of day-to-day security, domestic peace, respect for law and justice. It became possible to conceive of 'perpetual peace'. Even though many of the great liberal thinkers understood the connection between state consolidation and war, they also anticipated that increasing interchange between states and growing accountability of states towards an informed public could usher in a more integrated Europe and a more peaceful world, an extension of civil society beyond national borders. It was Kant, after all, who pointed out in 1795 that the global community had shrunk to the point where a 'right violated anywhere could be felt everywhere'. [13]

Clausewitz and the Wars of the Nineteenth Century

Clausewitz began to write *On War* in 1816, one year after the ending of the Napoleonic Wars. He had participated in the war on the losing side and had been taken prisoner, and the book is profoundly influenced by his experience. The Napoleonic Wars constituted the first people's war. Napoleon introduced conscription, the *levée en masse*, in 1793, and in 1794 he had 1,169,000 men under arms – the largest military force ever before created in Europe.

The central thesis of *On War*, particularly the first chapter which was the only chapter Clausewitz considered to be completed, is that war tends towards extremes. War is composed of three levels – the level of the state or the political leaders, the level of the army or the generals, and the level of the people. Roughly speaking, these three levels operate through reason, chance and strategy, and through emotion. From this trinitarian depiction of war, Clausewitz derived his concept of absolute war. Absolute war is best interpreted as a Hegelian abstract or ideal concept; it is the inner tendency of war that can be derived from the logic of the three different levels. It has its own existence, which is in tension with empirical realities.

The logic was expressed in terms of three 'reciprocal actions'. At a political level, the state always meets resistance in achieving its objectives and therefore has to press harder. At a military level, the aim has to be disarmament of the opponent in order to achieve the political objective, otherwise there is always a danger of counterattack. And, finally, the strength of will depends on popular feelings and sentiments; war unleashes passion and hostility that may be uncontrollable. For Clausewitz, war was a rational activity even though emotions and sentiments were mobilized in its service. In this sense, it is also a modern activity based on secular considerations and not confined by prohibitions derived from pre-rational conceptions of the world.

Real war differs from abstract war for two main reasons – political and military. First, the political objective may be limited and/or popular backing may be insufficient:

The more violent the excitement which precedes a war, by so much nearer will the war approach to its abstract form so much the more will it be directed to the destruction of the enemy so much the nearer will the military and political ends coincide so much the more purely military and less political the war appears to be but the weaker the motives and the tensions so much the less will be the natural direction of the military element – that is

force – be coincident with the direction which the political element indicates, so much the more must, therefore, the war become diverted from its natural direction.[14]

Second, war is always characterized by what Clausewitz calls
'friction' – problems of logistics, poor information, uncertain
weather, indiscipline, difficult terrain, inadequate organization
and so on – all of which slow down war and make it different in
reality from paper plans. War, says Clausewitz, is a 'resistant
medium' in which uncertainty, inflexibility and unforeseen cir-
cumstance all play their part. Real war is the outcome of the
tension between political and practical constraints and the inner
tendency for absolute war.

As forces increased in scale, it became more and more difficult for organization and command to be carried out by a single
person. Hence there was a growing need for a strategic theory
which could provide the basis for a shared discourse about war
through which war could be organized. As Simkin puts it, there
was a need for a 'jargon' which could guide common military
doctrines and what later became known as standard operating
procedures.[15]

Clausewitz provided the basic building blocks of a body of
strategic thinking that was developed during the nineteenth and
twentieth centuries. The two main theories of warfare – attrition theory and manoeuvre theory – were initially developed in
On War along with his discussion of offence and defence and of
concentration and dispersion. Attrition theory means that victory is achieved by wearing down the enemy, by imposing on
the enemy a higher casualty rate or 'attrition rate'. Attrition
theory is usually associated with defensive strategies and with
high concentrations of force. Manoeuvre theory depends on surprise and pre-emption. In this case, mobility and dispersion are
important to create uncertainty and to achieve speed. As
Clausewitz pointed out, these two theories are necessarily com-
plementary. It is very difficult to achieve a decisive victory
through attrition. Yet at the same time, a strategy based on manoeuvre ultimately needs a superiority of force to be successful.

The most salient conclusion of *On War* is the importance of
overwhelming force and a readiness to use force. This apparently simple point was not obvious in the early nineteenth-
century context in which Clausewitz was writing. In the

eighteenth century wars were fought, by and large, prudently, in order to conserve professional forces. There was a tendency to avoid battle; defensive sieges were preferred to offensive assaults; campaigns were halted for the winter and strategic retreats were frequent. For Clausewitz, battle was the 'single activity of war'; it was the decisive moment, which he compared to cash payment in the marketplace. The mobilization of force and the application of force were the most important factors in determining the outcome of war:

> As the use of physical power to the utmost extent by no means excludes the cooperation of the intelligence, it follows that he who uses force unsparingly, without reference to the bloodshed involved, must obtain a superiority if his adversary uses less vigour in its application. The former then dictates the law to the latter and both proceed to extremities to which the only limitations are those imposed by the amount of counteracting force on each side.[16]

The Napoleonic model in which all citizens were mobilized was not to be repeated until the First World War. However, several developments during the nineteenth century brought the Clausewitzean version of modern war closer to reality. One was the dramatic advance in industrial technology which began to be applied to the military field. Particularly important was the development of the railway and the telegraph which enabled much greater and faster mobilization of armies; these techniques were used to great effect in the Franco-Prussian War, which ended with the unification of Germany in 1871. The mass production of guns, particularly small arms, was pioneered in the United States so that the American Civil War is often described as the first industrialized war. The development of military technology was one reason for the extension of state activity into the industrial sphere. The late nineteenth-century naval arms race marked the emergence of what was later to be described as the military-industrial complex in both Germany and Britain.

A second development was the growing importance of alliances. If overwhelming force was what mattered in war, then force could be augmented through alliances. By the end of the nineteenth century, alliances began to solidify – an important reason why the major powers were all drawn into the First World War.

A third important development was the codification of the
laws of war which began in the mid-nineteenth century with
the Declaration of Paris (1856), which regulated maritime com-
merce in wartime. In the American Civil War, a prominent
German jurist was employed to draw up the so-called Lieber
Code, which laid down the rules and basic principles for war on
land and treated the rebels as an international opponent. The
Geneva Convention of 1864 (inspired by Henri Dunant who
founded the International Red Cross), the St Petersburg Declaration of 1868, the Hague Conferences of 1899 and 1907, and
the London Conference of 1908, all contributed to a growing
body of international law concerning the conduct of war – the
treatment of prisoners, the sick and wounded, and non-
combatants, as well as the concept of 'military necessity' and
the definition of weapons and tactics that do not conform to this
concept. While these rules were not always followed, they contributed importantly to a delineation of what constitutes legitimate warfare and the boundaries within which unsparing force
could be applied. In a sense, they were an attempt to preserve
the notion of war as a rational instrument of state policy in a
context where the logic of war, the extremist tendencies of war
combined with growing technological capacities, were leading
to ever-increasing levels of destructiveness.[17]

To sum up, modern war, as it developed in the nineteenth
century, involved war between states with ever-increasing emphasis on scale and mobility, and an increasing need for 'rational'
organization and 'scientific' doctrine to manage these large con-
glomerations of force.

The Total Wars of the Twentieth Century

In Clausewitz's work, there was always a tension between
his insistence on reason and his emphasis on will and emotion.
Men of genius and military heroes are central characters in *On
War*; sentiments like patriotism, honour and bravery are part
of the fabric of the book. Equally significant, however, are his
conclusions about the instrumental nature of war, the importance of scale and the need for an analytical conceptualization
of war. Indeed, the tension between reason and emotion, art
and science, attrition and manoeuvre, defence and offence,

instrumentalism and extremism constitute the key components of Clausewitzean thought. This tension can be said to have reached breaking-point in the twentieth century.

First of all, the wars of the first half of the twentieth century were total wars involving a vast mobilization of national energies both to fight and to support the fighting through the production of arms and necessities. Clausewitz could not possibly have envisaged the awesome combination of mass production, mass politics and mass communications when harnessed to mass destruction. Nevertheless, war in the twentieth century has come as close as can be conceived to Clausewitz's notion of absolute war, culminating in the discovery of nuclear weapons which, in theory, could wreak total destruction without 'friction'. But at the same time, some of the characteristics of the new wars were anticipated in the total wars of the twentieth century. In a total war, the public sphere tries to incorporate the whole of society, thus eliminating the distinction between public and private. The distinction between the military and the civil, between combatants and non-combatants correspondingly starts to break down. In World War I, economic targets were considered legitimate military targets. In World War II, the term 'genocide' entered into legal parlance as a result of the extermination of the Jews.[18] On the Allied side, the indiscriminate bombing of civilians, creating a scale of devastation of genocidal proportions (even if it did not match the scale of extermination carried out by the Nazis), was justified on the grounds of breaking enemy morale – as 'military necessity', to use the language of the laws of war.

Second, as war involved more and more people, the justification of war in terms of state interest became increasingly hollow, if it ever had any convincing validity. War, as van Creveld points out, is a proof that men are not selfish. No individualistic utilitarian calculation can justify risking death. The main reason why mercenary armies were so unsatisfactory is that economic incentive is, of its nature, inadequate as a motivation for warfare. The same is true of 'state interest' – a concept that derives from the same school of positivistic thinking that gave rise to modern economics. Men go to war for a variety of individual reasons – adventure, honour, fear, comradeship, protection of 'home and hearth' – but socially organized legitimate violence needs a common goal in which the individual soldier can believe and which he shares with others. If soldiers are to be treated as heroes and not as criminals, then heroic justification is needed to mobilize their energies, to persuade them to kill and risk being killed.

In the First World War, patriotism seemed sufficiently powerful to demand sacrifice and millions of young men volunteered to fight in the name of King and Country. The terrible experience of that war led to disillusion and despair and an attraction to more powerful abstract causes – what Gellner calls secular religions.[19] For the Allied nations, World War II was literally a war against evil; whole societies were mobilized, knowing what war entailed in a way that their predecessors in World War I did not: the fight against Nazism and the protection of their own ways of life. They fought in the name of democracy and/or socialism against fascism. In the Cold War, the same ideologies were called upon to justify the ever-continuing arms race. To justify the threat of mass destruction, the Cold War was presented as a struggle of good against evil along the lines of the wartime experience. That this justification was either unconvincing or insufficient is probably the main explanation for the failure of post-war military interventions, particularly the American intervention in Vietnam and the Soviet intervention in Afghanistan. The obstacles to successful counterinsurgency have been extensively analysed, but the central point is that soldiers did not feel like heroes. These were faraway countries where the rights and wrongs of the situation were not self-evident. At best, those who participated in the wars felt like pawns in a game of high politics they could not comprehend and, at worst, like murderers. In the United States – although not in Russia, which was to repeat the same mistake in Chechnya – where political leaders are highly conscious of public opinion, this experience has led to a deep reluctance to risk American casualties. The consequence has been the development of strategies, largely based on air power in which force can be applied without risking loss of life on the American side, which Edward Luttwak calls 'Post-Heroic Warfare'.[20]

Gabriel Kolko, in his monumental work on twentieth-century warfare,[21] argues that wars are always started by a 'handful of men' who suffer from 'socially sanctioned blindness'. Political leaders operate within an elite consensus that excludes dissenters, and consequently this allows for the transmission of false information and misleading illusions about what a war involves. His argument offers strong support for the thesis that democracies are less likely to be involved in wars. Undoubtedly, more accountable leaders would be less likely to embark on impossible adventures. In the case of World War I, however, the blindness of political leaders seems to have been shared by ordinary men and women. In the case of World War II, at least in Britain, public opinion was probably more belligerent than the appeasing political leaders. But embarking on wars is only the beginning; what matters in sustaining war is the extent to which the goal of war is recognized by those who participate in the war as legitimate. War is a paradoxical activity. On the one hand, it is an act of extreme coercion, involving socially organized order, discipline, hierarchy and obedience. On the other hand, it requires loyalty, devotion and belief from each individual. What has become clear in the post-war period is that there are few causes that constitute a legitimate goal for war, for which people are prepared to die.

In fact, the idea that war is illegitimate already began to gain acceptance after the trauma of the First World War. The Kellogg–Briand Pact of 1928 renounced war as an 'instrument of policy' except in self-defence. This prohibition was reinforced by the Nuremberg and Tokyo trials in which German and Japanese leaders were prosecuted for 'planning aggressive war' and codified in the UN Charter. Nowadays, it does seem to have become widely accepted that the use of force is only justifiable either in self-defence or if it is sanctioned by the international community, in particular, the UN Security Council.

Third, the techniques of modern war have developed to a point of sharply diminishing utility. The great battleships of the late nineteenth century turned out to be more or less irrelevant in the First World War. What mattered was mass-produced firepower. World War I was a defensive war of attrition in which rows of young men, directed by generals schooled in nineteenth-century strategic thought to use force unsparingly, were mowed down by machine guns. Towards the end of the war, the introduction of tanks and aircraft enabled an offensive breakthrough which made possible the type of manoeuvre warfare which was to characterize World War II. In the post-war period, the increase in the lethality and accuracy of all munitions, at least in part due to the revolution in electronics, has greatly increased the vulnerability of all weapons systems. The weapons platforms

of World War II have become extraordinarily complex and expensive, thus diminishing their utility because of cost and
logistical requirements, combined with ever-diminishing improvements in performance.[22] The problems of mobilization and
inflexibility, and the risks of attrition, have been magnified in
the post-war period, making it almost prohibitive to mount a
major operation except against a clearly inferior enemy, as in
the Falklands/Malvinas war of 1982 or the Gulf operation of
1991.

The logical endpoint of the technological trajectory of modern war is, of course, weapons of mass destruction, particularly
nuclear weapons. A nuclear war would be one in which force is
applied in the extreme in a matter of minutes. But what rational
purpose could ever justify their use? In the post-war period, many
strategic thinkers have grappled with this problem. Do not nuclear weapons nullify the premise of modern warfare – state interest?[23]

Finally, in the post-war period, alliances have been rigidified
so that the distinction between what is internal and what is external is also eroded. Already in the Second World War, it became apparent that individual nation-states could not fight wars
unilaterally. This lesson was applied in the construction of the
post-war alliances. Integrated command systems established a
military division of labour in which only the superpowers had
the independent capacity to wage full-scale wars. Essentially,
European countries, in the post-war period, abandoned one of
the essential attributes of sovereignty – the monopoly of legitimate organized violence – and, at least in Western Europe, what
was effectively a transnational civil society was extended to a
group of nations. There is a widespread discussion about the
social science finding that democracies do not go to war with
each other.[24] Interestingly enough, what is not discussed is the
integration of military forces on a transnational basis which provides a practical constraint against war. Claus Offe makes a similar
point about the 1989 revolutions in Eastern Europe; the reason
they were so peaceful, he argues, was because of the integration
of military forces in the Warsaw Pact and this also explains the
Romanian exception.[25]

Outside the alliances, a network of military connections was
established through looser alliances, the arms trade, the provision of military support and training, creating a set of patron–

client relationships which also inhibited the capacity to wage war unilaterally. Since 1945, there have been very few inter-state wars and these (India and Pakistan, Greece and Turkey, Israel and the Arab states) were generally restrained by super-power intervention. The exception, which proves the rule, was the Iran–Iraq war. This war lasted for eight years and could be waged unilaterally because of the availability of oil revenues. Both sides learned the disutility of modern conventional war-fare. To quote van Creveld again:

> A million or so casualties later, the belligerents found themselves back at their starting points. The Iranians were taught that, in the face of massive firepower assisted by gas, their fanatic young troops would not be able to achieve a breakthrough except on the road to heaven. The Iraqis learnt that conventional superior-ity alone was incapable of inflicting a meaningful defeat on a large country with almost three times their own population. Both sides were constantly hampered by the fear that, should the flow of oil be seriously disrupted, their conflict would attract superpower intervention. Both wanted a cease-fire and were relieved when one was finally concluded.[26]

The erosion of the distinctions between public and private, military and civil, internal and external, also calls into question the distinction between war and peace itself. The Second World War was a total war, representing a fusion between war, state and society – a fusion which continued to characterize totalitar-ian societies. The Cold War sustained a kind of permanent war psychosis based on the theory of deterrence which is best en-capsulated in the slogan 'War is Peace' in Orwell's *Nineteen Eighty-four*. The Cold War kept alive the idea of war, while avoid-ing its reality. The maintenance of large standing armies inte-grated in military alliances, the continued technological arms race, and the levels of military spending hitherto never experi-enced in peacetime, were supposed to have guaranteed peace because no war of the stylized type described in this chapter broke out on European soil. At the same time, many wars took place all over the world, including Europe, in which more peo-ple died than in the Second World War. But because these wars did not fit our conception of war, they were discounted.

The irregular, informal wars of the second half of the twenti-eth century, starting with the wartime resistance movements and the guerrilla warfare of Mao Tse-tung and his successors represent the harbingers of the new forms of warfare. The actors, techniques and counter-techniques which emerged out of the cracks of modern warfare were to provide the basis for new ways of socially organizing violence. During the Cold War, their character was obscured by the dominance of the East/West conflict; they were conceived as a peripheral part of the central conflict. Even before the end of the Cold War, when the threat of another 'modern war' really began to recede, we began to become aware of what Luttwak calls the new bellicosity.

3

Bosnia–Herzegovina: A Case Study of a New War

The war in Bosnia–Herzegovina lasted from 6 April 1992 until 12 October 1995, when a ceasefire agreement, brokered by the US Assistant Secretary of State Richard Holbrooke, came into effect.[1] Some 260,000 people died and around two-thirds of the population were displaced from their homes. Violations of human rights took place on a massive scale, including forced detention, torture, rape and castration. Many historic monuments of incalculable value were destroyed.

The war in Bosnia–Herzegovina has become the archetypal example, the paradigm of the new type of warfare. There are many other wars in the world, as Boutros Boutros-Ghali insensitively pointed out to Sarajevans, when he visited the city on 31 December 1992. If human tragedies can be measured in numbers, it can even be asserted, as Boutros-Ghali did, that more terrible things have happened in other places.[2] But the war in Bosnia–Herzegovina has impinged on global consciousness the way no other recent war has done.

The war mobilized a huge international effort, including high-level political talks involving all the major governments, the humanitarian efforts of international institutions and NGOs, as well as far-ranging media attention. Individual careers were made or broken, world status in the post-Cold War era was, at least partially, determined – the dismal inadequacy of the EU foreign policy-making capacity, the floundering of the UN, the US comeback, the redefinition of Russia's role. The current massive involvement of NATO troops, as well as troops from Partnership for Peace countries, will have profound consequences both for the future of NATO and the institutional framework of European security and for the way in which we conceive of peacekeeping.

For these reasons, the war in Bosnia–Herzegovina is likely to turn out to be one of those defining events, in which entrenched political assumptions, strategic thinking and international arrangements are both challenged and reconstructed. While the Gulf War was significant as the first post-Cold War international crisis, the Bosnian crisis lasted longer and is more representative of wars of the 1990s. When the war began, the central actors in the so-called international community had not had time to adjust their inherited mindsets either about the character of war or about their perception of Yugoslavia. The international reaction was at best confused and sometimes stupid, at worst culpable for what happened. But during the war some attitudes changed, especially among those operating on the ground. A few far-sighted individuals, both from Bosnia itself and from within international institutions, were, in perhaps marginal ways, able to influence and encourage new ways of thinking. As the century draws to a close, much depends, perhaps Europe's future itself, on how far lessons will have been learned and even absorbed.

This chapter traces the deficiencies of inherited ways of perceiving the war and sets out the need for a new type of analysis in relation to political and military assumptions about why and how wars are fought in the turn-of-the-century context and the implications for international involvement.

Why the War was Fought – Political Goals

Bosnia–Herzegovina was the most ethnically mixed republic of former Yugoslavia; according to the 1991 census, the population consisted of Muslims (43.7 per cent), Serbs (31.4 per cent), Croats (17.3 per cent) and the remainder included Yugoslavs, Jews, Roma and people who described themselves in a variety of other ways such as 'giraffes' or 'lampshades'. In fact, around a quarter of the population were intermarried and, in urban areas, a secular pluralistic culture flourished. The main difference be-

tween the ethnic groups was religion – the Serbs were Orthodox and the Croats were Catholic. In the first democratic elections of November 1990, parties which claimed to represent the
different ethnic groups received over 70 per cent of the votes
and controlled the National Assembly. These parties were the
SDA (the Party of Democratic Action) which was the Muslim
nationalist party, the SDS (the Serbian Democratic Party) and
the HDZ (the Croatian Democratic Party). Although they prom-
ised during the election campaign that their aim was for the
three communities to live peacefully together, these three groups
became the parties to the conflict.

The political goals of the Bosnian Serbs and the Bosnian Croats,
backed by Serbia and Croatia, respectively, were 'ethnic cleansing'. This phenomenon has been defined by the UN Commission of Experts as 'rendering an area ethnically homogeneous
by using force or intimidation to remove from a given area persons from another ethnic or religious group.'³ They wanted to
establish ethnically homogeneous territories which would
eventually become part of Serbia and Croatia, and to partition
the ethnically mixed Bosnia–Herzegovina between a Serbian and
a Croat part. To justify these goals, they used the language
of self-determination which was drawn from the earlier
communist rhetoric about wars of national liberation in the
third world. The goal of the Bosnian government, which was
controlled by the Bosnian Muslims, was the territorial integrity
of Bosnia–Herzegovina, since Muslims were a majority in Bosnia–
Herzegovina and had most to lose from partition; from time to
time, the Bosnian government was prepared to consider a rump
Muslim state or ethnic cantonization.

Ethnic cleansing has been a characteristic of East European
nationalism in the twentieth century. The term was first used to
describe the expulsion of Greeks and Armenians from Turkey
in the early 1920s. Ethnic cleansing takes a variety of forms,
ranging from economic and legal discrimination to appalling
forms of violence. The milder form was practised by Croatia
after the elections of 1990 when Serbs began to lose their jobs
and when Serb policemen in Serb majority areas were replaced.
The form of violent ethnic cleansing that was to be typical of
the war in Bosnia–Herzegovina was initiated by the Serbs in
Croatia together with the JNA (the Yugoslav National Army),
and sundry paramilitary groups, systematized by the Bosnian

Serbs and their allies in Bosnia–Herzegovina, and copied by the Croats both in Bosnia–Herzegovina and in Croatia.

How is this form of virulent ethnic nationalism to be explained? The dominant perception of the war is expressed in the terms 'Balkanization' or 'tribalism'. The Balkans, it is argued, situated at the confluence of civilizations and caught historically between the shifting borders of the Ottoman and Austro-Hungarian empires, has always been characterized by ethnic divisions and rivalries, by ancient hatreds that persist just beneath the surface. These divisions were temporarily suppressed during the communist period, only to burst forth again in the first democratic elections. 'A Letter from 1920', a short story written by Ivo Andrić between the two world wars, is widely quoted as evidence for this view. In the story, a young man decides to leave Bosnia for ever, because it is 'a country of fear and hate'.[4]

This perception of the war, evident, for example, in David Owen's book, pervaded European policy-making circles and the high-level negotiations.[5] It was deliberately fostered by some of the parties to the conflict themselves. Thus Karadžić, the Bosnian Serb leader, said that Serbs, Croats and Muslims were like 'cats and dogs', while Tudjman, the Croatian president, repeatedly emphasized that Serbs and Croats could not live together because Croats were Europeans while Serbs were Easterners, like Turks or Albanians.[6] (Interestingly enough, he seems, at least from time to time, to think it is possible to live with Muslims since in his view they are really Croats, and Croatia and Bosnia–Herzegovina were traditionally united. On the other hand, the Serbs consider Muslims to be like Turks, in other words, like themselves according to Croat conceptions!)

It is a view which corresponds to the primordial view of nationalism, that nationalism is inherent and deeply rooted in human societies deriving from organically developed 'ethnies'.[7] What it does not explain is why there are long periods of coexistence of different communities or nationalities, nor why waves of nationalism take place at particular times. It does not explain the undoubted existence of alternative conceptions of Bosnian and indeed Yugoslav society as a rich unified culture, as opposed to multiculturalism, which includes the various religious communities and languages and also important elements of secularity.[8] Undoubtedly, Bosnia–Herzegovina has a grim history, especially during the twentieth century, but so do other parts of

Europe. The view that aggressive nationalism is somehow pecu-
liar to the Balkans allows us to assume that the rest of Europe is
immune to the Bosnian phenomenon. The former Yugoslavia,
despite the fact that it was earlier considered to be the most
liberal of the communist regimes and first on the list of potential
new members of the EU, has become a black spot in the middle
of Europe surrounded by other supposedly more 'civilized' societies – Greece to the south, Bulgaria and Romania to the east,
Austria, Hungary and Italy to the north and west. But what if
the current wave of nationalism has contemporary causes? Does
not the primordial view amount to a kind of myopia, an excuse
for inaction, or worse?

There is an alternative view which holds that nationalism has
been reconstructed for political purposes. This view corresponds
more closely to the 'instrumentalist' conception of nationalism,
according to which nationalist movements reinvent particular
versions of history and memory to construct new cultural forms
that can be used for political mobilization.[9] What happened in
Yugoslavia was the disintegration of the state both at a federal
level and, in the case of Croatia and Bosnia–Herzegovina, at a
republican level. If we define the state in the Weberian sense as
the organization which 'successfully upholds the monopoly of
legitimate organized violence', then it is possible to trace first
the collapse of legitimacy and, second, the collapse of the monopoly of organized violence. The emergence of virulent nationalism, which did indeed construct itself on the basis of certain
traditional social divisions and prejudices – divisions which by
no means encompassed the whole of contemporary Yugoslav
society – has to be understood in terms of the struggle, on the
part of increasingly desperate (and corrupt) elites, to control the
remnants of the state. Moreover, in a post-totalitarian society,
control is much more extensive than in more pluralistic societies, extending to all major social institutions – enterprises,
schools, universities, hospitals, media and so forth.

To understand why the state ruptured along national lines
can be best explained in terms of the recent history of Yugoslavia rather than by delving into the pre-communist past. The
Titoist regime was a totalitarian regime in the sense of centralized control over all aspects of social life. It was more liberal
than other regimes in Eastern Europe; it allowed a certain degree of economic pluralism; from the 1960s Yugoslav citizens

were allowed to travel and hold foreign currency accounts; artistic and intellectual freedom was much greater than in other communist countries. The political identity of the Yugoslav regime was derived, in part, from the struggle of the partisans during World War II; in part, from its capacity to provide reasonable living standards for the population; and, in part, from its special international position as a bridge between East and West, with its own indigenous brand of socialism, and its role as leader of the non-aligned movement. As the memory of World War II faded and as the economic and social gains of the post-war period began to disappear, it was inevitable that its legitimacy would be called into question. The fall of the Berlin Wall, the democracy movements in the rest of Eastern Europe, and the end of the East / West division added a final blow to former Yugoslav identity.

Although the Yugoslav partisans had fought on the slogan 'Brotherhood and Unity' and the aim was to develop a new socialist Yugoslav man or woman, as in the Soviet Union, the regime had built into its functioning a complicated system of checks and balances to ensure that no ethnic group became dominant; in effect, it institutionalized ethnic difference. In order to counterbalance the numerical dominance of Serbs, six republics were established, each (with the exception of Bosnia–Herzegovina) with a dominant nationality – Serbia, Montenegro, Croatia, Bosnia–Herzegovina, Slovenia and Macedonia. In addition, there were two autonomous provinces inside Serbia – Kosovo (where there was an Albanian majority) and Vojvodina (with a mixed population of Serbs, Croats and Hungarians). Despite this, polls consistently showed, up until the 1980s, growing support for Yugoslavism. This system was augmented by the 1974 constitution which devolved power to republics and autonomous provinces and established a mechanism for elite rotation based on ethnic arithmetic. Although the League of Communists retained its monopoly position, after 1974 the party itself increasingly divided along national lines. In a situation in which other political challenges were disallowed, a nationalist political discourse became the only form of legitimate debate. In effect, there were ten communist parties – one for each republic and autonomous province, one for the federation and one for the JNA. As Ivan Vejvoda points out, the 1974 constitution empowered collective actors, notably *nomenklatura* at the republican and provincial levels, while further disenfranchising individual citizens. It was decentralization of totalitarianism.[10] In this context, national communitarian identities were the obvious candidates to fill the vacuum created by the loss of Yugoslavism.

Yugoslavia experienced the strains of economic transition some ten years earlier than other East European countries.[11] During the 1950s and 1960s, the country experienced fast economic growth based on a model of rapid defence-oriented heavy industrialization that was typical of centrally planned economies. In the Yugoslav case, this was somewhat modified by the self-management model and the fact that agriculture, for the most part, remained in private hands. During this period, Yugoslavia received substantial amounts of foreign assistance because it was seen as a buffer against a possible Soviet attack on Southeast Europe. In the 1970s, Western aid began to decline and was replaced by commercial loans, which were relatively easy to acquire following the oil crisis. As in the case of other centrally planned economies, Yugoslavia had great difficulty restructuring its economy; this was compounded by the slowdown in growth in Western countries, which inhibited the growth of exports and reduced the earnings from remittances from Yugoslavs working abroad, and by the growing autonomy of the republics and autonomous provinces who felt no responsibility for the balance of payments and competed with each other to create money.

By 1979, the debt had reached crisis proportions – some $US 20 billion. An International Monetary Fund (IMF) Recovery Plan was agreed in 1982 which included both liberalization and austerity. The main effect of this plan was to intensify the competition for resources at the level of the republics and to contribute to the growing criminalization of the economy. The federation was unable to control the creation of money and by December 1989, the monthly inflation rate had reached 2500 per cent. Unemployment averaged 14 per cent throughout the decade; particularly hard hit were urban middle classes largely dependent on state salaries and pensions, and rurally based industrial workers who were forced to survive on what they could produce from their small agricultural plots. A series of corruption scandals in the late 1980s, especially in Bosnia–Herzegovina, revealed the growing links between the degenerate ruling elite and a new class of mafia types. Typical in this respect was the

Agromerc scandal which revealed the nefarious activities of Fikret Abdić, long time party boss in Bihac, who was later to become a key figure in the war. Nationalist arguments were a way of coping with economic discontent, appealing to the victims of economic insecurity and concealing the growing *nomenklatura*–mafia alliance.

By the end of the 1980s the unravelling of Yugoslav statehood had gathered pace. The last federal Prime Minister, Antje Marković, tried to reimpose control at a federal level with a programme of 'shock therapy' introduced in January 1990. Despite the success of the programme in reducing inflation, it caused immense resentment at the level of republics because it effectively removed their 'license to print money'.[12] By November 1990, Yugoslavia as a single economic space was challenged by various unilateral economic actions – above all, massive Serbian borrowing to pay for the imposition of Serbian rule in Kosovo known as the 'Great Bank Robbery', but also the Slovene refusal to contribute to the Fund for Underdeveloped Regions, and the unilateral Croatian abolition of excise tax on cars effectively bribing voters with the promise of cheaper foreign cars.

Yugoslavia as a single communicative space unravelled alongside the unravelling of the economy. By the 1970s, each republic and province controlled its own television and radio. There was occasional rotation of news programmes on the first channel and news from other republics and autonomous provinces could be seen (by rotation) on the second channel. This broke down in the late 1980s.[13] Despite the last-ditch attempt by Marković to establish an all-Yugoslav television, *Yutel*, the media were effectively nationalized, providing a powerful basis for nationalist propaganda.

By 1990 federal legitimacy had been challenged, at the level both of legislatures and of the judiciary. The first democratic elections were held in the republics and not at a federal level. When the federal constitutional court challenged decisions taken by the newly elected republican parliaments, such as the Slovene decision not to contribute to the Fund for Underdeveloped Regions or the Slovene and Croatian declarations of sovereignty, these legal opinions were ignored. A similar disregard for constitutional decisions taken at a republican level was shown by those Serbs in Croatia who wanted to declare a 'Serbian Autonomous Region'.

Finally, the last vestige of Yugoslav statehood was removed in 1991, when the monopoly of organized violence broke down. The JNA had been the bastion of Yugoslavism.[14] Already by the 1970s Territorial Defence Units (TOs) were established in the republics as a result of a new 'Generalized Popular Defence System' introduced after the Soviet invasion of Czechoslovakia in 1968. By 1991 the JNA was increasingly being used as a tool of Slobodan Milošević, the President of Serbia, while the Slovenes and Croats were secretly organizing and arming their own independent forces based on the TOs and the police through the growing black market for surplus arms then emerging in Eastern Europe. At the same time, the Serbs were creating their own paramilitary groups. In particular, they initiated their plan 'RAM' (Frame), secretly to arm and organize the Serbs in Croatia and Bosnia–Herzegovina. The JNA utterly failed in its efforts to disarm the paramilitaries (the Croats and Slovenes claimed that their forces were not paramilitary groups but legal defence forces) and ended up siding with the Serb paramilitary groups in Croatia and Bosnia.[15]

The emergence of a new form of nationalism paralleled the disintegration of Yugoslavia. It was new in the sense that it was associated with the disintegration of the state in contrast to earlier 'modern' nationalisms which aimed at state-building and that, unlike earlier nationalisms, it lacked a modernizing ideology. It was also new in terms of the techniques of mobilization and the forms of organization. It was Milošević who was the first to make extensive use of the electronic media to propagate the nationalist message. His 'anti-bureaucratic revolution', which aimed to remove the Titoist system of checks and balances perceived as discriminating against Serbs, provided the basis for a populist political appeal over the heads of the existing communist hierarchy. Through mass rallies, he legitimized his hold on power. The victim mentality often characteristic of majorities who feel themselves minorities was nurtured with an electronic diet of tales of 'genocide' in Kosovo, first by the Turks in 1389 and more recently by the Albanians, and of holocaust in Croatia and Bosnia–Herzegovina, with clips of the Second World War interspersed with current developments. In effect, the Serbian public experienced a virtual war long before the real war was to take place – a virtual war that made it difficult to distinguish truth from fiction so that war became a continuum in which the 1389 battle of Kosovo, the Second World War and the war in Bosnia were all part of the same phenomenon. David Rieff describes how Bosnian Serb soldiers after a day of shooting from the hills around Sarajevo would ring their Muslim friends in the town. This extraordinarily contradictory behaviour made perfect sense to the soldiers because of the psychological dissonance produced by this virtual reality. They were not shooting at their private friends, but at Turks. 'Before the summer ends', one soldier told Rieff, 'we will have driven the Turkish army out of the city, just as they drove us from the field of Kosovo in 1389. That was the beginning of Turkish domination of our lands. This will be the end of it, after all these cruel centuries . . . We Serbs are saving Europe even if Europe does not appreciate our efforts.'[16]

If Milošević perfected the media technique, it was Tudjman who developed the horizontal transnational form of organization. Unlike Milošević, he came from a dissident background, having spent time in prison in the early 1970s for his nationalist views, although formerly he had been a JNA general. His party – the HDZ – had little time to prepare for the first democratic elections, and did not control the media. Tudjman, however, had been mobilizing support among the Croatian diaspora in North America. He claimed that the HDZ had branches in thirty-five North American cities, each with fifty to several hundred members and some with up to two thousand members. The diaspora was always regarded with great suspicion by the Communist authorities; émigrés were largely considered to be former *Ustashe* (the wartime Croatian fascists). Tudjman said later that the most crucial political decision he had ever made was to invite the émigrés back for the HDZ Congress in February 1990.[17] This transnational form of organization was a highly significant source of funds and election techniques, and, subsequently, arms and mercenaries. It induced another form of virtual reality arising from the time–space distantiation of diaspora party members, who were, in effect, imposing on a contemporary situation an image of Croatia which dated from when they had left.

The process of disintegration and the rise of a new form of virulent nationalism was encapsulated in Bosnia–Herzegovina, which had always been a mixed society. The differentiation of communities along religious lines (Orthodox, Catholic, Muslim and Jewish) had been institutionalized during the latter part of Ottoman rule through the millet system and, in various forms, this 'institutionalised communitarianism', as Xavier Bougarel calls it,[18] was sustained throughout Austro-Hungarian rule (1878–1914) and during the first and second Yugoslavias. Nevertheless, in the post-war period there were many mixed marriages and, particularly in cities, the communitarian logic was supplanted by a modern secular culture. Yugoslavism was particularly strong in Bosnia–Herzegovina. It was in this republic that *Yutel* was most popular and that Marković was to choose to launch his reform party.

Bougarel distinguishes 'institutionalised communitarianism' from political and territorial nationalism. The former depends on a balance between communities which is known as *komšiluk* (good neighbourliness) and which is threatened by political or military mobilization as happened during the two world wars. The re-emergence of political nationalism in the late 1980s occurred, as was the case earlier, for instrumental reasons. It was a response, according to Bougarel, to discontent arising from uneven development and to the growing divide between the economic and scientific elite and backward rural regions. This divide was especially acute in Bosnia–Herzegovina and was exacerbated during the 1980s. It was also a response to the loss of legitimacy of the ruling party.

Six months before the 1990 elections, a poll conducted in Bosnia–Herzegovina showed that 74 per cent of the population favoured the banning of nationalist parties. Yet when the election did take place, 70 per cent of the voters supported these parties. This discrepancy can be explained in terms of Bougarel's argument. Most people feared the threat to *komšiluk* represented by the nationalist parties. But once political mobilization took place, they found it necessary to rally to their community. Even so, other factors also need to be taken into account. On the one hand, the League of Communists in Bosnia–Herzegovina was traditionally considered hard line and slow to adapt to the wave of pluralism that was affecting the rest of Eastern Europe – the nationalist parties represented the most obvious alternative to the communists. Moreover, it was discredited by a series of corruption scandals in the late 1980s. On the other hand, the speed of nationalist mobilization is explained partly by the role of Croatia and Serbia. The HDZ, the Croat nationalist party, was actually a branch of Tudjman's party, and the SDS, the Serb nationalist party, was a branch of the Serbian nationalist party that was established in the Krajina, the Serb-dominated part of Croatia. In addition, *Matica Hrvatska*, the Croatian cultural centre in Zagreb, and the Serbian Academy of Sciences, responsible for the notorious 1986 memorandum which first set out a Serb nationalist programme, both played an active role in mobilizing nationalist sentiment, together with the religious institutions.

The elections were won by the nationalist parties and they formed an uneasy coalition – not surprisingly, given the conflicting nature of their political goals. In particular, the SDS members of the Assembly were repeatedly outvoted by the SDA and the HDZ. The non-nationalist civic parties won 28 per cent of the vote; they were supported largely by urban intellectuals and industrial workers. The war was precipitated by the decision of the international community to recognize Slovenia and Croatia and any other former Yugoslav republic provided it held a referendum and recognized minority rights (something that was ignored in the Croatian and Bosnian cases). The SDA and HDZ favoured independence; the Serbs did not.

Bougarel concludes that the contradictory portrayals of Bosnia–Herzegovina as a land of tolerance and coexistence and as a country of fear and hate are, in fact, both true. Fear and hate are not endemic but, in certain periods, are mobilized for political purposes. The very scale of the violence can be interpreted not as a consequence of 'fear and hate', but rather as a reflection of the difficulty of reconstructing 'fear and hate'. As Živanović, an independent-minded liberal who remained in Serb-controlled areas throughout the war, put it: 'The war had to be so bloody because the ties between us were so strong'.[19] This mobilization of 'fear and hate' takes specific forms in specific periods and has to be explained in terms of specific causes. In other words, the new nationalism is a contemporary phenomenon arising from recent history and shaped by the current context.

It is sometimes argued that Muslim nationalism is a different phenomenon from Serb and Croatian nationalism. Those who oppose the dominant perception of the war as a civil war often argue that this was a war of Serbian and, to a lesser extent, Croatian aggression. It is certainly true that Bosnian Serb nationalists, aided and abetted by the Serbian and Yugoslav governments, were the aggressors in this war, and it was they who initiated and applied most systematically and extensively the policy of ethnic cleansing. Likewise, Croat nationalists, backed by the Croatian government, followed their example, albeit on a lesser scale. It is also the case that the SDA, the Muslim nationalist party, was always in favour of a unified multicultural Bosnia–Herzegovina. However, multiculturalism, for the Muslim nationalists, meant political organization along communitarian lines – hence, Izetbegović's attempts to organize 'acceptable' ethnic groupings such as the Serb Civic Council or the Croat Peasants' Party. Moreover, the SDA did display some of the tendencies of other nationalist parties – such as the tendency to impose rigid political control over all institutions, or the use of the media to generate a virtual war against other communities: the SDA magazine, *Dragon of Bosnia*, has been especially shrill in its calls for nationalist violence.[20] The UN Commission of Experts says that Bosnian forces did not engage in ethnic cleansing, although they committed war crimes. However, Croatians were certainly expelled or chose to leave from parts of Central Bosnia captured by Bosnian forces during the Muslim–Croat conflict, and this was also true of Serbs in areas captured during the last days of the war. In other words, this was a war of Serbian and Croatian aggression, but it was a new nationalist war as well.

That fear and hate were not endemic to Bosnian society became apparent in the outburst of civic activism during the run-up to the war.[21] A mass peace movement developed with strong support from the Bosnian media, trade unions, intellectuals, students and women's groups. Tens of thousands of people formed a human chain across every single bridge in Mostar in July 1991. A *Yutel*-organized rally in Sarajevo in August 1991 was attended by 100,000 people. In September, 400 European peace activists, travelling as the Helsinki Citizens Assembly Peace Caravan, joined thousands of Bosnians in a human chain which linked the Mosque, the Orthodox Church, the Catholic Church and the Synagogue in Sarajevo. Similar demonstrations were organized in Tuzla and in Banja Luka and other towns and villages.

The highpoint and the end of the movement came in March and April 1992. On 5 March, peace activists succeeded in pulling down barricades erected by Muslim and Serb nationalist groups after a Serb bridegroom had been shot at his wedding. On 5 April, 50 –100,000 demonstrators marched through Sarajevo to the parliament building to demand the resignation of the government and to ask for an international protectorate. Thousands more came in busloads from Tuzla, Zenica and Kakanj but could not enter the city because of Serb and Muslim barricades. The war began when Serb snipers fired on the demonstrators from the Holiday Inn – the first person to die was a twenty-one-year-old medical student from Dubrovnik.[22] The following day, Bosnia–Herzegovina was recognized by European states and the Serbs left the Bosnian Assembly. The state was recognized at the very moment of its disintegration.

According to Bougarel, the Bosnian war was a civil war in the sense that it was a war *against* the civilian population and *against* civil society.[23] And Tadeusz Mazowiecki, the Special Rapporteur for the UN Commission on Human Rights, reports the belief of some observers that 'the attacking forces are determined to "kill" the city [Sarajevo] and the tradition of tolerance and ethnic harmony that it represents'.[24] Or to put it another way, the war could be viewed as a war of exclusivist nationalists against a secular multicultural pluralistic society.

How the War was Fought – Military and Economic Means

Yugoslavia was probably the most militarized country in Europe outside the Soviet Union. Until 1986, military spending amounted to 4 per cent of GNP – more than any other non-Soviet European country except Greece.[25] The JNA itself consisted of some 70,000 regular officers and staff, plus around 150,000 conscripts. In addition, each republic and autonomous province was responsible for organizing and equipping the TOs, largely reserve forces, which were reportedly one million strong.

The JNA remained a Yugoslav entity up to 1991. The army controlled a network of interconnected bases, weapons stores and enterprises, which, in contrast to the rest of the economy, were organized on a Yugoslav-wide basis. Even though the partisan strategy which informed JNA organization was based on decentralized local combat formations, control remained centralized at a Yugoslav level. Among JNA officers, 70 per cent of whom were Serbian or Montenegrin, Yugoslavism continued to grow at a time when it was declining in other spheres of social life. The JNA accounted for the bulk of the federal budget and, by 1991, it seemed as though the JNA and the League of Communists were virtually all that was left of the Yugoslav idea

– hence, Yugoslavism came to be associated with totalitarianism and militarism.

From 1986 to 1991 military spending fell dramatically, from $US2,491 million in constant 1988 prices to $US1,376 million,[26] thus contributing to a growing sense of victimization and paranoia about internal and external enemies within the JNA. (The arrest of young Slovenian journalists who had criticized arms exports to the third world in 1988, and the subsequent notorious trial, was an expression of this paranoia.) The story of the wars in Slovenia, Croatia and, above all, Bosnia–Herzegovina, is also the story of the break-up of the Yugoslav military-industrial complex. The JNA and the TOs disintegrated into a combination of regular and irregular forces augmented by criminals, volunteers and foreign mercenaries competing for control over the former Yugoslavia's military assets.

At the outset of the war in Bosnia–Herzegovina, there was a bewildering array of military and paramilitary forces. In theory, there were three parties to the conflict – the Serbs, Croats and Bosnians. In practice, different forces cooperated with each other in differing combinations throughout the war. Thus, in the early stages of the war, the Croats and Bosnians cooperated against the Serbs. Then, after the publication of the Vance–Owen Plan in 1993, which was based on ethnic cantonization, the Croats and Muslims started fighting each other, since the Croats wanted to establish control of 'their' cantons. Then came the Washington Agreement between the Muslims and Croats, imposed by the Americans, and, in the final stages of the war, the Muslims and Croats cooperated again, at least officially. During the course of the war, the forces of each party to the conflict were increasingly centralized and regularized. By the end of the war, the main regular forces were the Bosnian Serb Army (BSA), the Croatian Defence Council (HVO) and the Army of Bosnia–Herzegovina (ABiH).

After the ten-day war in Slovenia in June 1991, the JNA withdrew to Croatia (leaving their weapons behind). By mid-July 1991, the JNA had moved an estimated 70,000 troops into Croatia. Together with some 12,000 irregular Serb forces, both local volunteers and (often criminal) groups imported from Serbia proper, they experimented with the strategies that were to be used in Bosnia–Herzegovina. After the ceasefire in Croatia, the JNA withdrew to Bosnia–Herzegovina taking with them their equipment. In May 1992, the JNA formally withdrew from

Bosnia–Herzegovina. In practice, only some 14,000 troops withdrew to Serbia and Montenegro; approximately 80,000 troops transferred to the Bosnian Serb Army.

The HVO was formed out of the militia attached to the HDZ. It operated together with the Croatian army (HV), which was formed on the basis of Croatian territorial defence forces and built up during the course of the war with training assistance from a private company formed by American retired generals called Military Professional Resources Incorporated (MPRI).[27]

There was no Bosnian army when the war broke out. Essentially, the defence of Bosnian territory was locally organized. Sarajevo was defended by a motley crew of patriotic leagues and other paramilitary groups, largely organized by the Sarajevo underground. Tuzla was defended by the local police force augmented by a locally organized patriotic league. Although Izetbegović announced the formation of a regular army in May 1992, it was not until Silajdžić became Prime Minister in the autumn of 1993 that the various gangster groups were controlled and the army command was centralized. Even at that time, the UN Commission of Experts estimated that of 70,000 troops only 44,000 were armed.[28]

The BSA was much better equipped than the other regular forces, as can be seen from table 3.1. In particular, it had a considerable advantage in heavy weapons – tanks, artillery, rocket launchers and mortars. It inherited the JNA's equipment and, more importantly, it controlled most of the JNA's weapons stores, which had been situated in the hills of Bosnia–Herzegovina because this was envisaged to be the heartland of any guerrilla-based defence of Yugoslavia and which had been well stocked in anticipation of a long war. The ABiH, which was the least well equipped, and suffered, in particular, from a dearth of heavy weapons, was dependent on Croatian supply routes to acquire arms.[29] The HVO received equipment from Croatia. In addition to equipment taken from weapons stocks in Croatia, various black-market sources were used to acquire mainly surplus ex-Warsaw Pact equipment. (Interestingly, there was some evidence that ex-JNA enterprises in Croatia, Slovenia and Serbia continued to cooperate to produce spare parts and equipment.[30])

In addition to the regular forces, it is possible to identify three main types of irregular force: paramilitary organizations, generally under the control of an individual; foreign mercenary groups;

Table 3.1   *Regular forces in Bosnia–Herzegovina 1995*

	Armed forces	Main battle tanks	Artillery	Multiple rocket launchers	Mortars
ABiH	92,000	31	100	2	200
HVO	50,000	100	200	30	300
BSA	75,000	370	700	70	900

Source: *Military Balance 1995–6*, International Institute for Strategic Studies, London, 1996

and local police augmented by armed civilians. The UN Commission of Experts identified eighty-three paramilitary groups on the territory of former Yugoslavia – some fifty-six were Serbian, thirteen were Croatian and fourteen were Bosnian. The estimated size of these forces was 20–40,000, 12–20,000 and 4–6,000 respectively. The vast majority of these acted locally, but certain groups operated much more widely in conjunction with regular forces and gained considerable notoriety.

On the Serb side, the two most well-known groups were Arkan's 'Tigers' and Šešelj's Chetniks or 'White Eagles'. Arkan, whose real name was Željko Ražnjatović, was a big figure in the Belgrade underworld. He owned a string of ice-cream parlours which were allegedly a cover for his smuggling activities, which expanded considerably during the war. Before the war, he had apparently been recruited by a special unit in the Yugoslav government in order to assassinate émigrés. He also owned the fan club of the Belgrade Red Star football team and his Tigers were recruited from the club. The Tigers initially operated in Croatia; in Bosnia–Herzegovina they were reported as operating in twenty-eight counties. According to reports collected by the UN Commission: 'Their hair was cut short and they wore black woollen caps, black gloves cut off mid-finger, and black badges on the upper arm. According to other reports, they wore multi-coloured uniforms, red arrows, knit caps, a badge showing the Serbian flag on the right arm, and an emblem showing a tiger and the words "Arkanove delije" on the shoulder.'[31] The Tigers were well armed, including tanks and mortars.

Šešelj had been a dissident. He had taught at the University of

Sarajevo and, reportedly, spent a year at the University of Michigan.[32] He was imprisoned in the early 1980s for his anti-communist writings. After he was released, he moved to Belgrade, where he joined the Serbian nationalists. His party, the Serbian National Renewal Party, gained seats in the 1990 elections and was particularly successful in the federal elections of May 1992, when he won 33 out of 138 seats. Like the Tigers, the Chetniks were initially active in Croatia. In Bosnia–Herzegovina, they were reported to operate in thirty-four counties. The Šešeljovci were 'bearded men'. They wore Serbian military berets with a Serbian military flag on the front, or black fur hats with a Serbian cockade. They were reportedly always drunk and they recruited additional 'weekend fighters'.

Both Arkan and Šešelj seem to have operated together with the JNA. According to the UN Commission: 'In many of these counties, Šešelj and Arkan exercised control over other forces operating in the area. These forces consisted of local paramilitary groups, and sometimes the JNA. In some counties, Šešelj's and Arkan's forces operated under the command of the JNA.'[33] Šešelj always insisted that his forces were armed and equipped by Milošević.

The most well-known Croatian paramilitary group was HOS, a wing of the Croatian Party of Rights (HSP). Its members wore black uniforms and the Croatian chequered shield like the wartime *Ustashe*. Up to 1993, when their leader Dobroslav Paraga was arrested for trying to overthrow the Croatian government, HOS operated in conjunction with the HVO. Another Croatian paramilitary group was the 'Wolves' led by Jusuf Prazina, known as Juka. He was an underworld figure from Sarajevo before the war broke out and had been in prison five times. The Wolves wore 'crew-cuts, black jump-suits, sun glasses and sometimes masks'.[34] They operated together with the ABiH until August 1992 and then worked with the HVO.

The two notorious gangsters Ćaco and Ćelo operated in Sarajevo up until the autumn of 1993. Ćaco had been a club musician called Musan Topalović, and Ćelo was a criminal who had just come out of prison after serving eight years for rape. Most paramilitary groups on the Bosnian side were referred to as Green Berets or Muslim Armed Forces (MOS) and reportedly operated under the command of the ABiH.

The names of other paramilitary groups include Black Swans,

Yellow Ants (which referred to their looting abilities), Mečet's Babies, Mosque Pigeons, Knights, Serbian Falcons and so on.

Among mercenaries, the most well-known were the *Mujahidiin*, mostly veterans from the Afghan war. They have been expelled under the Dayton Agreement. They reportedly operated in Zenica, Travnik, Novi Travnik, Mostar and Konjic. According to Croat intelligence, they were organized by a man named Abdulah, who owned the 'Palma' video shop in Travnik. The UN Commission suggests that the *Mujahidiin* acted more or less independently of the ABiH. Other mercenaries included the Garibaldi Unit (Italians fighting alongside the Croats), Russians fighting on the Serbian side, as well as mercenaries from Denmark, Finland, Sweden, Britain and the United States. British soldiers made redundant in the post-Cold War cuts took up positions training both Bosnian and Croatian forces.

Local militia were organized by municipalities as in Tuzla, or by big enterprises as in Velika Klusa, Fikret Abdić's Agromerc, or in Zenica, where the former communists still controlled the steelworks.

During the war, the formal economy collapsed. This was the result of a combination of factors: physical destruction, impossibility of acquiring inputs, and loss of markets. Industrial production was estimated at 10 per cent of its pre-war level and unemployment was between 60 and 90 per cent. The currency collapsed; exchange was based on a combination of barter and deutschmarks. For the most part, people faced a painful choice: they could live insufficiently off humanitarian aid; they could volunteer for the army or become a criminal or both; or they could try to leave. Many people left, especially the young and educated, so that the population decline was even more dramatic than the figures on ethnic cleansing suggest.

The various military forces were totally dependent on outside sources of assistance. These included direct support from outside governments, 'taxation' of humanitarian assistance, and remittances from individuals. The regular forces were largely funded and equipped by sponsor governments. The BSA was funded by the Serbian government up to the embargo, imposed by Milošević in August 1994. The HVO was funded by Croatia, and the ABiH received support from Islamic states and, covertly, from the USA. The paramilitaries were funded from loot and extortion of expelled people, as well as confiscation of equipment, etc. from conquered territories, 'taxation' of humanitarian aid which they collected at many checkpoints, and the black market. The local militia were funded by municipalities who received the 'taxes' from humanitarian assistance collected on their territory and also continued to tax citizens, including those who were abroad, and enterprises on their territory. All three types of force cooperated with each other both militarily and economically.

The strategy adopted by this combination of regular and irregular forces – a strategy practised most consistently and systematically by the Bosnian Serbs as well as by the Bosnian Croats – was territorial gain through political control rather than military offence. Violence was used to control populations rather than to capture territory. The difficulty of acquiring territory through military offence was made plain quite early on in the war in Croatia. The JNA experienced the classic problems of offence which have become typical of modern war, as was illustrated by the Iran–Iraq war. The two-month siege of Vukovar, a town in East Slovonia, Croatia, from September to October 1991, showed how massive superiority in both firepower and manpower was insufficient to capture a relatively small town. When Vukovar eventually fell on 20 November 1991, it had been reduced to rubble. The attempt to take Dubrovnik, which, according to the memoirs of the then Minister of Defence, General Kadijević, was part of a plan to occupy Split and the Dalmatian Coast, failed.[35] A characteristic feature of the war in Bosnia was the siege of the main Bosnian cities. Although they could not be captured, they could be shelled continuously and cut off from supplies.

Except in the early stage of the war in Bosnia–Herzegovina, when the Bosnian Serbs faced very little opposition and, in the last stages of the war when they had become very weak, little territory changed hands. Essentially, the war was directed not against opposing sides, but against civilian populations. This explains why there was no continuous front. Instead, different areas were controlled by different parties, and forces were interspersed in what the UN Commission describes as a 'chequered' military map, with confrontation lines in and around cities encircling the areas of control. Indeed, in late 1993, before the Washington Agreement between Muslims and Croats, territory under Bosnian control basically consisted of a few enclaves surrounded by hostile forces, what some described as a 'leopard skin' territory. With the exception of Banja Luka, which was under Serb control, and Mostar, which was divided between Croats and Muslims, most towns remained under Bosnian control while the countryside was divided between Serbs and Croats.

Apart from a few strategic points, e.g. the Brcko corridor which connected Serb territories and which potentially provided a communication route from Northern Bosnia to Zagreb, there was relatively little fighting between the opposing sides. There were, indeed, various examples of cooperation, mostly in the black market, but also differing short-term and local military cooperation between different parties. On one occasion, UNPROFOR (the United Nations Protection Force) intercepted a telephone conversation between the local Muslim Commander in Mostar and the local Serb Commander discussing the price in German marks to be paid if the Serbs would shell the Croats. The nadir was reached when the Serbs took Mount Igman, overlooking Sarajevo, in July 1993; the paramilitary groups at that time defending Mount Igman were ready to 'sell' their positions in order to control the black-market routes. Most of the violence was directed against civilians – the shelling of cities and towns combined with sniper fire and various forms of atrocity within the towns and villages – and became, in effect, what was known as ethnic cleansing.

The Bosnian Serbs wanted to create an autonomous Bosnian Serb territory. But since there were almost no areas except Banja Luka where Serbs were numerically dominant and, perhaps more importantly, extremist Serbs were numerically dominant, this had to be brought about through ethnic cleansing. The areas seem to have been chosen for strategic reasons, to link the Serb-held territories in Krajina with Serbia, and to control JNA bases and weapons stores. The tactic of establishing 'Serb autonomous areas' seems to have followed a consistent pattern first worked out in the war in Croatia. Descriptions of the process can be found in numerous reports of journalists, UN agencies and independent NGOs such as Helsinki Watch.

The typical pattern applied to rural areas – villages and small towns. First, the regular forces would shell the area and issue frightening propaganda so as to instil a mood of panic. Reports of terror in neighbouring villages would add to the panic. Then the paramilitary forces would close in and terrorize the non-

Serb residents with random killing, rape and looting. Control over local administration would then be established. In the more extreme cases, non-Serb men were separated from the women and taken to detention centres. Women were robbed and/or raped and allowed to go or taken to special rape detention centres. Houses and cultural buildings such as mosques were looted, burned or blown up. The paramilitary groups also seem to have had lists of prominent people – community leaders, intellectuals, SDA members, wealthy people – who were separated from the rest and executed. 'It was the conscious elimination of an articulate opposition and of political moderation. It was also the destruction of a community from the top down.'[36] The television journalist Michael Nicholson refers to this process as 'elitocide' and the Mayor of Tuzla talks about 'intellectual cleansing'.

The existence of detention centres became known in August 1992. The UN Commission of Experts identified some 715, of which 237 were operated by Bosnian Serbs, 89 by the ABiH and government and 77 by Bosnian Croats. According to the Commission, they were the scene of 'the worst inhumane acts', including mass executions, torture, rape and other forms of sexual assault. (Although grave breaches of the Geneva Conventions were reported in the Bosnian camps, the allegations were fewer and less systematic than in the Serbian and Croatian camps.) A specific aspect of the process of ethnic cleansing has been widespread rape. Although mass rape has taken place in other wars, its systematic character, in detention centres and in particular places and at particular times, suggests that it may have been part of a deliberate strategy.[37]

In urban areas, in particular Banja Luka, ethnic cleansing was a slower, more legalistic process. The lives of non-Serbs were made untenable. For example, they were removed from their jobs, with no access to medical care; communication was cut off; they were not allowed to meet in groups of more than four. In many towns, variously described Bureaux for Population Exchange were established through which non-Serbs or non-Croats could surrender their property and pay large sums to be allowed to leave.[38]

Similar techniques were adopted in Croat-controlled areas. In Bosnian-controlled areas the evidence does not suggest deliberate ethnic cleansing, although many non-Muslims, especially Serbs, left for a variety of reasons, including psychological pressure, discrimination and forced recruitment in the army.[39] By the end of 1995, ethnic cleansing was almost complete, as can be seen from table 3.2. Only 13,000 Muslims remained in Northern Bosnia, according to UNHCR estimates, out of an original population totalling around 350,000, and only 4,000 Muslims and Croats remained in East Bosnia and South Herzegovina, out of an original population totalling 300,000. Many Serbs and Croats had also left Tuzla and Zenica.

The worst atrocities, certainly in the early stages of the war, seem to have been committed by paramilitary groups. According to the UN Commission: 'There is a . . . strong correlation between reports of para-military activity and reports of rape and sexual assault, detention facilities and mass graves. These types of activity (i.e. para-military activity and grave breaches of the Geneva Conventions) tended to occur in the same counties and evidence the localised nature of the activity.'[40] On the Serbian side, the activities of Arkan and Šešelj are well known; the UN Commission suggests that these were coordinated with the activities of the JNA (BSA), whereas, on the Croatian and Bosnian sides, the paramilitary groups acted more independently of regular forces. On the Croatian side, Paraga is said to have organized the detention camps at Capljina and Dretelj, while Juka was reported to have killed some 700 Muslims in Mostar and was responsible for the detention camp at the heliport.[41] On the Bosnian side, the worst atrocities seem to have been committed by the *Mujahidiin*.

The motivation of the paramilitary groups seems to have been largely economic, although there were clearly nationalist fanatics among them. According to Vasić, around 80 per cent of the paramilitaries were common criminals and 20 per cent were fanatical nationalists: 'The latter did not last long (fanaticism is bad for business).'[42] Arkan, reportedly, had lists of rich Muslims in possession of gold and money. The 'right to be the first to loot' was viewed as a form of payment.[43] Many former criminal groups were able to expand their pre-war rackets; most of the paramilitary groups were involved in black-market activities and, indeed, cooperated with each other across supposed confrontation lines in order to profit from the situation in besieged enclaves. Effectively, paramilitary groups were 'hired' to do the dirty work necessary to instil the 'fear and hate' which was not yet endemic in Bosnian society. Thus, the mafia economy was

Table 3.2 *Ethnic cleansing in Bosnia–Herzegovina*

	1991 census				Estimates November 1995[a]			
	Serbs	*Croats*	*Muslims*	*Total*	*Serbs*	*Croats*	*Muslims*	*Total*
Bihac	29,398	6,470	202,310	238,178	1,000	5,000	174,000	180,000
Northern Bosnia–Herzegovina	624,840	180,593	355,956	1,161,389	719,000	9,000	13,000 [38,000 in Dec 94]	741,000
Zenica	79,355	169,657	328,644	577,656	16,000	115,000	439,000	570,000
Tuzla	82,235	38,789	316,000	437,024	15,000	19,000	659,000	693,000
Sarajevo	157,526	35,867	259,085	432,478	n/a	n/a	n/a [629,000]	455,000
Enclaves	20,000		80,000	100,000			50,000 [115,000]	50,000
West Herzegovina/West-Central Bosnia	43,595	245,586	111,128	400,309	5,000	320,000	160,000	485,000
East Bosnia/South Herzegovina	304,017	40,638	261,003	605,658	450,000	4,000[b]	see previous column	454,000
Total	1,340,966	717,600	1,655,300	3,972,692	1,206,000 (−Sarajevo)	470,000	1,497,000	3,628,000

Figures in square brackets show numbers in November 1994.

[a] These figures are almost certainly overestimates, since more than a million Bosnian refugees left the country.

[b] This figure refers to both Croat and Muslim communities.

n/a Not available.

Source: UNHCR, Information Notes on Former Yugoslavia 11/95, Zagreb, 1995.

built into the conduct of warfare, creating a self-sustaining logic to the war both to maintain lucrative sources of income and to protect criminals from legal processes which might come into effect in peacetime.

The situation was better in a few places where the local state apparatus survived. One example was Tuzla, where the non-nationalists had won the 1990 elections. Tuzla was defended by the local police and local volunteers, who later became a local brigade of the Bosnian army, and an ideology of multicultural civic values was vigorously promoted. Throughout the war, the city maintained local energy sources and some local production including mining. At the height of the war, when the town was completely cut off, the people lived off humanitarian assistance and rent in kind from UNPROFOR. By the end of the war, taxes raised in Tuzla accounted for 60 per cent of the total tax revenue of the Bosnian government. Nevertheless, it has proved very difficult for these islands of relative civility to survive in what Bougarel calls the communitarianized predatory economy.[44]

Towards the end of the war, the local militia and paramilitary groups were absorbed into the regular armies. The former became local brigades and the latter became 'Special Units'. The capture of Srebrenica, a classic ethnic-cleansing operation, in July 1995 was entirely carried out by the BSA. On the third day, the Special Units were sent in to do their usual bit. On all sides, there were failed attempts to create a mobilization economy. In particular, after Serbia imposed a blockade on the Bosnian Serbs in August 1994, the BSA was reduced to self-finance. The Bosnian Serb government tried to centralize finance and take control of key sectors but this was rejected by the so-called Serb parliament, whose members were linked in to the criminal economy. On all sides, but especially the Serb side, morale was very low at the end of the war. Vasić suggests that the BSA only had 30,000 effective troops. Many people, especially young people, had left; poverty, criminality and indiscipline were rife.

How far was the strategy of ethnic cleansing planned in advance? Or was it chanced upon by Serb forces in Croatia? The UN Commission says that the JNA's Department of Psychological Operations was reported to 'have had several plans for local provocation by special forces controlled by the Ministry of the Interior and "ethnic cleansing" '.[45] It quotes an article in the Slovenian newspaper *Delo* which claimed that along with the plan 'RAM' (to arm the Serbs in Croatia and Bosnia–Herzegovina) the JNA had an additional plan for mass killings of Muslims and mass rapes as a weapon of psychological warfare: 'Analysis of the Muslims' behaviour showed their morale, desire for battle, and will could be crushed most easily by raping women, especially minors and even children, and by killing members of the Muslim nationality inside their religious facilities.'[46]

It is sometimes suggested that the JNA drew on its history as a partisan movement. It is certainly true that the localized and decentralized nature of the war has many parallels with guerrilla warfare. The organization of TOs meant that many trained reservists could be drawn into the war at a local level and that small arms in local weapons caches were easily available. However, in many ways, ethnic cleansing is the exact opposite of guerrilla warfare, which depended on the support of the local population; the guerrilla was supposed to be the 'fish in the sea', to use Mao's words. The aim of ethnic cleansing was the wholesale destruction of communities, the manufacture of 'fear and hate'. One speculation is that JNA thinking was perhaps influenced by counterinsurgency doctrines, as developed by the Americans in Vietnam and tried out in the low-intensity conflicts of the 1980s. Alex de Waal has suggested that African military strategists were influenced by these doctrines, and this may, in part, explain the similarities of the Bosnian war to the wars in Africa.[47] Undoubtedly, JNA staff would have studied these wars. The last Yugoslav Minister of Defence, General Kadijević, had spent six months at West Point Military Academy, although counterinsurgency was only a minor part of the curriculum there, and other JNA officers had also studied in the United States. It is probably more convincing to argue that the strategy of ethnic cleansing was developed on the ground, although prior discussions and experience must have had some relevance.

It was not only members of other ethnic groups who were targeted in the strategy of ethnic cleansing. It was moderates as well, those who refused to hate. This was first learned in Croatia when Babić and Martić, the leaders of the Krajina Serbs, seized control of the town of Pakrac and removed Serbs as well as people of other nationalities in positions of authority. Throughout the war, there have been people on all sides who refused to be drawn into the mire of 'fear and hate'. The reports of the Special Rapporteur for the UN Commission on Human Rights consistently notes the actions of brave Serbs who tried to protect their Muslim and Croat neighbours. The *Guardian* newspaper reported a Serb 'Schindler' living in Prijedor who organized his friends and neighbours to protect Muslims. The Jewish community in Mostar organized itself to help Muslims escape. Even though their ranks have been greatly depleted by death and flight, non-nationalist groups and parties still exist in different parts of Bosnia–Herzegovina.

The Nature of International Involvement

From the beginning, international involvement in the war in Bosnia–Herzegovina, and indeed in all the conflicts on the territory of former Yugoslavia, was extensive. This involvement took place both at an official level and at the level of civil society. The war became the focus of media attention and of peace, humanitarian and human rights groups, as well as of civic institutions like churches or universities. Within the former Yugoslavia, great hopes were vested in the role of the international community. For many people, the term 'Europe' had an almost mystical significance; it was considered synonymous with civilized behaviour and emblematic of an alternative 'civic' outlook to which those who opposed nationalism aspired. What actually happened was deeply disappointing, giving rise to cynicism and despair.

In fact, there were two quite distinct forms of international involvement. One was the high-level political talks and missions. The other was, in effect, a new form of humanitarian intervention. The latter, I would argue, did in fact represent a considerable innovation in international action both in its goals and in its scale and in the way it fostered cooperation between international institutions and civil society. But it was fatally thwarted by the contradictions between what was happening at a humanitarian level and what was happening at the level of high politics, and, connectedly, by misconceptions about the political and military nature of the war.

There have been many explanations for the failure of the international community to prevent or stop the wars in the former Yugoslavia – lack of cohesion in the EU, unwillingness of governments to provide adequate resources, the short-termism of politicians. All these explanations have something in them. But the fundamental problem was conceptual, the failure to understand why or how the war was fought and the character of the new nationalist political formations that emerged after the collapse of Yugoslavia. Both politically and militarily, the war was perceived as a conflict between competing nationalisms of a traditional essentialist type, and this was true both of the Europeans who, like the Serbs, argued that the nationalisms were all equally to blame, and of the Americans, who tended to see the Serbs as bad 'totalitarian' nationalists and the Croats and Muslims as good 'democratic' nationalists. While Serbian and Croatian nationalism was definitely bad nationalism and Muslim nationalism was not quite so bad, such an analysis missed the point that this was a conflict between a new form of ethnic nationalism and civilized values. The nationalists had a shared interest in eliminating an internationalist humanitarian outlook, both within the former Yugoslavia and globally. Both politically and militarily, their war was not against each other but, to repeat the argument of Bougarel, against the civilian population and against civil society.

The so-called international community fell into the nationalist trap by taking on board and legitimizing the perception of the conflict that the nationalists wished to propagate. In political terms, the nationalists had a common totalitarian goal: to reestablish the kind of political control the Communist Party had once enjoyed on the basis of ethnic communities. To this end, they had to partition society along ethnic lines. By assuming that 'fear and hate' were endemic to Bosnian society and that the nationalists represented the whole of society, the international negotiators could see no other solution but the kind of compromise which the nationalists themselves aimed to achieve. By failing to understand that 'fear and hate' were not endemic but were being manufactured during the war, they actually contributed to the nationalist goals and helped to weaken the internationalist humanitarian outlook.

In military terms, it was assumed that the main violence was between the so-called warring parties, and that civilians were, so to speak, caught in the crossfire. While the evidence of ethnic cleansing was plain to see, this was treated as a side-effect of the fighting, not as the goal of the war. The UN troops that were sent to Bosnia–Herzegovina to protect the civilian population were hamstrung because their masters were so fearful of being dragged into a conventional war. A sharp distinction was drawn between peacekeeping and war-fighting. Peacekeeping meant that the troops operated on the basis of consent between the warring parties. War-fighting would have meant taking sides. Throughout the war, the fear that any use of force would mean taking sides and would escalate the international military involvement prevented UN troops from effectively carrying out the humanitarian tasks they were sent to perform. What was not understood was that there was rather little fighting between the sides in the conventional sense and that the main problem was the continuing violence against civilians. The UN troops were supposed to be peacekeeping troops; they operated on the basis of consent. The consequence was that they were unable to protect aid convoys or safe havens; instead, they stood by, as one Sarajevan wag put it, 'like eunuchs at the orgy'.

The predominant approach in the high-level talks was an approach 'from above', a *realpolitik* approach, in which it was assumed that the leaders of political parties spoke for the people they represented. The problem of how to deal with the debris of Yugoslavia was thus understood as a problem of reaching a compromise with those leaders. Essentially, the problem was conceived as a problem of borders and territory, not as a problem of political and social organization. Since ethnic cleansing was seen as a side-effect of the war, the main concern was to stop the fighting by finding a political compromise acceptable to the warring parties. If the political leaders in the former Yugoslavia insisted that they could not live together, then some new set of territorial arrangements had to be found for the post-Yugoslav political space. Hence, the answer was partition. But partition was a cause of war as much as a solution. It was self-perpetuating since, as everyone knew, there was no way to create ethnically pure territories without population displacement. Since ethnic cleansing was the goal of the war, the only possible solution was one which accepted the results of ethnic cleansing. Thus, the very principle of partition legitimized nationalist claims.

The first partition was that of Yugoslavia, when Slovenia and Croatia, and later Bosnia–Herzegovina, were recognized.[48] At the same time, Croatia was partitioned after the ceasefire negotiated by Cyrus Vance, the UN envoy, in December 1991. The recognition of Bosnia–Herzegovina took place on the day that war broke out. In the efforts to halt the fighting, a series of doomed plans to partition Bosnia–Herzegovina were put forward, culminating in the Dayton Agreement. The first plan was the Carrington–Cuteleiro Plan of the spring of 1992, which proposed to partition Bosnia–Herzegovina in three parts. After the failure of this plan, Lord Carrington resigned as EU negotiator and was replaced by David Owen, who became joint Chairman with Cyrus Vance of the International Conference on Former Yugoslavia (ICFY) established after the London Conference in August 1992. The Vance–Owen Plan was considered to be an improvement on the Carrington–Cuteleiro Plan because it divided Bosnia–Herzegovina into ten cantons, nine of which were based on the domination of one or other of the ethnic groups. The plan was eventually rejected by the Bosnian Serb Assembly in May 1993, but not before it had provided the legitimation for the Croats to ethnically cleanse the regions they were awarded under the plan – this marked the beginning of the Croat–Muslim conflict. (It was said that HVO stands for 'Hvala Vance Owen' – Thank you Vance Owen.) Under pressure from the Americans, a Muslim–Croat ceasefire was negotiated in the spring of 1994; essentially, the Washington Agreement, as the ceasefire agreement was known, established a Bosnia–Croat federation partitioned into even smaller ethnically dominated cantons. Meanwhile, the Vance–Owen Plan was replaced by the Owen–Stoltenberg Plan (Cyrus Vance having been replaced by Thorvald Stoltenberg), which was in turn supplanted by the Contact Group Plan – the Contact Group being a new negotiating forum involving the major outside players (the USA, Russia, Britain, France and Germany). Both these plans and the Dayton Agreement that eventually succeeded in halting the fighting were very similar to the original Carrington–Cuteleiro Plan.

The Dayton Agreement finally succeeded in bringing about a ceasefire, partly because of military pressure (NATO finally undertook air strikes and an Anglo-French Rapid Reaction Force was sent to Bosnia), partly because of the collapse of Bosnian Serb morale, and perhaps most importantly because the military situation on the ground had been 'rationalized', with the Serb capture of two of the Eastern enclaves and the Croatian capture of the Krajina.[49] In other words, ethnic cleansing was virtually complete. Such was the ease of the military endgame that it has been suggested that there may have been some tacit understanding between Serbia and Croatia, perhaps even encouraged by outside players.[50] Certainly, the eventual partition was close to what Milošević and Tudjman had discussed way back in March 1991, at a famous meeting in Karadjordjevo.[51]

The problem with partition is that it entrenches the new form of nationalism and can only be sustained through force. The situations in the Serb-controlled areas of Croatia, before they were captured by the Croatian government, within the Croat–Muslim federation after the Washington Agreement, and in the whole post-Dayton Bosnia–Herzegovina are very similar. There is less killing; the unbearable tension of daily vulnerability to shelling and sniper fire is lessened. However, the nationalists remain in power; evictions and violations of human rights continue; freedom of movement is restricted, as are political freedoms; the mafia economy continues to function. Moreover, there is an ever-present threat of renewed war since the absence of war has a tendency to weaken the effectiveness of the nationalist narrative.

The negotiators were strongly criticized for even talking to the warring parties. How could they be seen to shake hands with people named as war criminals? How could they treat Izetbegović, the President of a recognized country, on a par with the Bosnian Serbs and the Bosnian Croats?[52] Those engaged in the negotiations make the point that those who make the war are the only ones who can stop it and therefore there are no alternatives to talks between the warring parties. There is something in this argument, but these talks should not have been given the priority they received in the overall policy. There were ways in which the non-nationalist political and civic parts of Bosnian society could have been given access to governments and international institutions, in which their ideas and proposals, including proposals for alternatives to partition, could have been heard and taken seriously and in which they were publicly seen to have the respect of the international community. They represented the hope for international values; they should have been seen as the main partners in the search for peace. There was an utter failure to understand that the nationalists did not and could not, because of the nature of their goals and the way in which they were pursued, appeal to 'hearts and minds', and that it was of vital importance to foster an alternative.

In parallel with the high-level talks was the humanitarian

intervention. At an early stage in the conflict, Mrs Ogata, the High Commissioner for Refugees, put forward a seven-point humanitarian response plan which was accepted by governments and international agencies in July 1992. The seven points were: 'respect for human rights and humanitarian law, preventive protection, humanitarian access to those in need, measures to meet special humanitarian needs, temporary protection measures, material assistance, and repair and rehabilitation.'[53] UNHCR took the lead role in a massive humanitarian effort providing aid to around two-thirds of the population of Bosnia–Herzegovina, and it coordinated the activities of a range of international humanitarian agencies and NGOs. Many courageous individuals contributed to this effort as aid workers, medical personnel, convoy drivers, etc. In addition to the aid effort, a series of measures were adopted by the UN aimed at protecting the civilian population and upholding international humanitarian law. These included the decision to protect humanitarian convoys, by force, if necessary (Security Council Resolution (SCR) 770 (1991)); the declaration of safe areas (SCR 836 (1993)); the appointment of a Special Rapporteur for Human Rights by the Commission on Human Rights (August 1992); the appointment of a Commission to investigate war crimes (October 1992) and, in particular, rape (December 1992); and the establishment of 'an international tribunal for the prosecution of persons responsible for serious violations of international humanitarian law' (SCR 808 (1993)). The International Committee of the Red Cross (ICRC) was charged with gaining access to detention camps and organizing prisoner releases. And in the Washington Agreement, an EU administration was established to administer Mostar with the aim of reuniting the city.

These measures, at least in theory, represented a very significant innovation in international practice. Adopted under pressure from the international media, which exposed the reality of the war, and from campaigning groups, they constituted a potential new form of international humanitarianism. Although elements of the package had been introduced in previous conflicts – the safe haven/area concept in Iraq, the protection of humanitarian convoys in Somalia – this was the most ambitious deployment of UN peacekeeping troops designed to assist and protect the civilian population and to uphold humanitarian law. Moreover, the wording of the relevant Security Council resolutions were strong. Both SCR 770 (1992), which called for protection for humanitarian convoys and unimpeded access for the ICRC and other humanitarian organizations to 'camps, prisons and detention centres', and SCR 836 (1993), which established safe areas, were under Chapter VII of the UN Charter which authorizes the use of force.[54] Some 23,000 UNPROFOR troops were sent to Bosnia–Herzegovina.

In addition to the UNPROFOR troops, NATO and the Western European Union (WEU) maintained naval forces in the Adriatic monitoring the arms embargo, and NATO was responsible for enforcing the No Fly Zone over Bosnian air space, which was also authorized under Chapter VII (SCR 816 (1993)).

However, almost none of these measures was effectively implemented. Humanitarian aid was constantly obstructed and 'taxed' by the warring parties. The safe areas became vast insecure refugee camps constantly subjected to shelling; humanitarian supplies were controlled sadistically by the Bosnian Serbs. War crimes continued to be committed, despite the efforts of Mazowiecki, the UN Commission of Experts and the Tribunal, the ICRC and other humanitarian organizations – indeed some of the worst instances of ethnic cleansing occurred in the last few months of the war. The No Fly Zone was violated on countless occasions and the arms embargo was never strictly maintained. Despite the EU administration, Mostar continued to be divided, freedom of movement was still restricted and numerous violations of human rights were recorded. Many UN personnel themselves engaged in black-market activities, and allegations of crimes committed by UN personnel, especially rape, were never properly investigated. The nadir for the UN came in July 1995, when the so-called safe areas of Srebrenica and Zepa were overrun by Bosnian Serb forces.

Was any other approach possible once the war had begun? In political terms, David Owen argues that the first priority was to stop the fighting. But even now, after Dayton, it can be asked whether an agreement would ever have been reached before the parties were ready for it and whether the role of the international negotiators was anything more than a way of facilitating and legitimizing an agreement which, at least, the Serbs and the Croats wanted to reach. The consequence is that it is now extremely hard, as has already become clear, to dislodge the nationalists and war criminals from power, making long-term peace or normality a distant prospect.

Had the war been understood as, first and foremost, a war of genocide, then the first priority would have been the protection of the civilian population. Negotiations and political pressure could have focused on concrete goals on the ground to ease the humanitarian situation – such as the opening of Tuzla airport or the Mount Igman route to Sarajevo, or the release of prisoners – rather than on partition. The inclusion of non-nationalist parties and groups in the negotiation process could have assisted this task and made possible other take-it-or-leave-it overall solutions not based on partition such as an international protectorate.[55] At the very least, such an approach would have strengthened the alternatives to nationalism, thus obstructing the manufacture of 'fear and hate', and would have left the legitimacy of international organizations more intact. On several occasions, Mazowiecki complained about the lack of cooperation with ICFY: 'The Special Rapporteur requested that human rights concerns should have priority in the peace process, and pointed out that peace negotiations should not have been conducted without ensuring the cessation of massive and gross human rights violations.'[56]

Militarily, a different perception might have led to a tougher, more 'robust' approach to peacekeeping. The belief that this was a war with 'sides' led to an extreme timidity about the use of force for fear that this would escalate and drag the international community into the war on one side or another. General Michael Rose was obsessive about crossing what he called the 'Mogadishu line', in reference to the failure of the UN mission in Somalia. It can, with equal justice, be argued that a tougher approach would have made the task easier and UN forces and personnel much less vulnerable than they were to hostage-taking or sporadic attacks. When in 1993 British soldiers, escorting a relief convoy to Tuzla from Kladanj, started to shoot back at Serbs firing from the hills, harassment was dramatically reduced. Yet General Morillon, the then Commander of UNPROFOR troops in Bosnia–Herzegovina, was reprimanded by the UN Secretary General for 'exceeding his mandate'. A similar story can be recounted when a Danish officer in Tuzla ordered a tank to fire on the Serbs in retaliation for shelling.

For those on the ground, the frustration was immense, both for the UNPROFOR personnel themselves who were being ordered to appear to be cowards and for the personnel of humanitarian organizations who found their task as difficult as it had been before the arrival of the UN troops. Since humanitarian passage had to be negotiated anyway, this could as easily be done by the sheer willpower of people like UNHCR's Larry Hollingsworth or Gerry Hulme than by a toothless UNPROFOR. As Larry Hollingsworth pointed out when leaving Bosnia:

> If you send in an army but don't allow it to be aggressive, why send in firepower and tanks? I'm left sadly with the conclusion that the troops were sent in not to be tough but to look tough . . . We should have been much tougher from the beginning. The UN missed the chance to seize the initiative and be forceful, and we have seen a gradual chipping away of authority ever since.[57]

Owen himself argues that tougher peacekeeping was impossible because there were insufficient troops. He points out that it is impossible, for example, to defend the 55-mile route from Sarajevo to Goradze which crosses two mountain ranges, forty-four bridges and two narrow ravines: 'Calls for "robust" or "muscular" action from politicians, retired generals and commentators in television studios were greeted with hollow laughs from the men on the ground.'[58] But the argument can be put the other way round. The troops were equally, if not more, vulnerable if they were not prepared to use force, and this was clearly understood by the warring parties; hence, the temptation to expose this and to humiliate the international community by, for example, hostage-taking. Tougher action would have required regrouping and refusal to undertake certain tasks, for example monitoring as opposed to destroying heavy weaponry.

For similar reasons, Owen is very dismissive of the safe haven/area concept. It is true that UNPROFOR originally asked for 30,000 troops to defend the safe areas and argued that, at a pinch, they could make do with 10,000. In the end the Security Council authorized 7,500 troops, but money was only appropriated for 3,500 troops. The problem was that this argument was used to explain why nothing could be done, instead of intensifying the pressure for more troops. Towards the end of the war, increasing pressure from individuals such as General Morillon or Mazowiecki as well as public opinion did lead eventually to the deployment of the Rapid Reaction Force on Mount

Igman and the toughening of the rules of engagement for the Implementation Force (IFOR).

In the end, the main use of force was air strikes, which had always been advocated by the Americans because they are a way of using force without risking casualties. Operation Deliberate Force lasted from 29 August to 14 September 1995; in all, 3,515 sorties were flown and more than 1,000 bombs were dropped.[59] Air strikes did help to put pressure on the Bosnian Serbs as a prelude to the Dayton Agreement and, supposedly, they deterred an attack on the last Eastern enclave, Goradzc. But air strikes are a cumbersome instrument for protecting civilians on the ground, and it was the protection of civilians that was needed above all else. Many people argue that the deployment of the Rapid Reaction Force was more effective.

What was needed, in effect, was not peacekeeping but humanitarian law-enforcement. This does represent a considerable challenge. It requires new strategic thinking about how to counter strategies of population control through ethnic cleansing – how to develop support and promote alternative sources of legitimacy among the local population, new rules of engagement and norms of behaviour, appropriate equipment, forms of organization and command structures.

After Dayton

The longest and most destructive war in Europe since 1945 ended after three and a half years. The international operation mounted to implement the peace agreement involved an array of international institutions – the UN, the EU, the Council of Europe, the OSCE, NATO and the WEU. For NATO, IFOR and its successor, the Stabilization Force (SFOR), is the largest ever military operation undertaken by the Alliance. Moreover, NATO is working together with the Partnership for Peace countries, formerly members of the Warsaw Pact. In the process of implementation, political assumptions, military norms as well as the 'architecture' of international institutions, are likely to be determined for the foreseeable future.

The Dayton Agreement exhibited all the contradictions that have dogged international involvement from the start of the war in Bosnia. It was primarily an agreement borne of the

realpolitik approach of high-level negotiators who perceive the
world as divided into primordial nations. It was an agreement
which partitioned Bosnia and Herzegovina into three 'entities'
and in which the 'parties to the agreement' – i.e. the nationalists – were primarily responsible for its implementation. Nevertheless, the agreement also contained clauses which commit
the parties, including the international community, to a humanitarian approach – clauses about human rights, the prosecution of war criminals, the return of refugees, freedom of
movement, economic and social reconstruction. Effectively, the
agreement grants considerable power to the NATO commanders and to the High Representative responsible for civic implementation, which, if utilized effectively and in conjunction with
those groups and parties within Bosnia who still stand for civic
values, could yet reintegrate the country. This is difficult, however, because of the way the Dayton Agreement legitimizes
the warring parties.

   These two approaches suggest two scenarios for the future
shape of Europe. The first is the partition scenario in which
peace is equated with the legitimation of authoritarian nationalist regimes and the role of international institutions, under
the weakened leadership of the United States, with sporadic
intervention to keep ongoing conflicts more or less under control. Peacekeeping, in this instance, consists of a more or less
forceful separation of warring parties. This is not just a scenario for the former Yugoslavia or even Eastern Europe. It could
eventually apply to all of Europe and, indeed, beyond, because
of what such an approach would do to undermine the appeal
of internationalism. This has been called the 'Latin American
scenario'.[60]

   The second scenario is based on the humanitarian approach.
It would envisage cooperation among international institutions
and civic groups both in Bosnia and elsewhere to build a political and social alternative to nationalism. This would mean taking seriously the civic components of the agreement, particularly
the enforcement of internal security – i.e. respect for human
rights and prosecution of war criminals – as well as building,
through social and economic reconstruction, an alternative to
the mafia economy, and encouraging and assisting the return
of refugees. Peacekeeping, in this instance, means enforcement
of humanitarian law. If Bosnia has become the paradigm of the

new type of warfare and was metaphorically thrown out of Europe, it could also become a model for a new type of humanitarian reconstruction and a symbol of a new Europeanism or internationalism.

4

The Politics of New Wars

During the war in Bosnia–Herzegovina, Sarajevo was divided territorially between a Serb-controlled part and a Bosnian (mainly Muslim) part. But wartime Sarajevo could also be described in terms of a non-territorial divide. There was a group of people who could be described as the globalists – UN peacekeepers, humanitarian agencies, journalists and Sarajevans who spoke English and were employed as assistants, interpreters and drivers. They were able to move freely in and out of the city and across the territorial divide protected by armoured cars, flak jackets and blue cards. At the same time, there were also the local territorially-tied inhabitants of the city. On one (the Bosnian) side, they were under siege for the duration of the war, living off humanitarian aid or the black market (if they were lucky enough to have deutschmarks), prey to sniper fire and occasional shelling. On the other (Serb) side, material conditions were somewhat better, although the climate of fear was worse. On both sides, they were vulnerable to the press gang and the various militias and mafia-types who roamed the streets and claimed legitimacy in terms of the national struggle.

The political goals of the new wars are about the claim to power on the basis of seemingly traditional identities – nation, tribe, religion. Yet the upsurge in the politics of particularistic identities cannot be understood in traditional terms. It has to be explained in the context of a growing cultural dissonance between those who participate in transnational networks which communicate through e-mail, faxes, telephone and air travel, and those who are excluded from global processes and are tied to localities even though their lives may be profoundly shaped by those same processes.

It would be a mistake to assume that this cultural divide can be expressed in simple political terms, that those who support particularistic identity politics are reacting against the processes of globalization, while those who favour a more tolerant, multicultural universalistic approach are part of the new global class. On the contrary, among the globalists are to be found diaspora nationalists and fundamentalists, 'realists' and neo-liberals who believe that compromises with nationalism offers the best hope for stability, as well as transnational criminal groups who profit from the new wars. And while there are many among the territorially tied who are likely to cling to traditional identities, there are also courageous individuals and citizens' groups who refuse particularisms and exclusiveness.

The point is rather that the processes known as globalization are breaking up the cultural and socio-economic divisions that defined the patterns of politics which characterized the modern period. The new type of warfare has to be understood in terms of this global dislocation. New forms of power struggle may take the guise of traditional nationalism, tribalism or communalism, but they are, nevertheless, contemporary phenomena arising from contemporary causes and displaying new characteristics. More-over, they are paralleled by a growing global consciousness and sense of global responsibility among an array of governmental and non-governmental institutions as well as individuals.

In this chapter, I describe some of the key characteristics of the process known as globalization and how they give rise to new forms of identity politics. In the last section, I shall try to outline the emerging political cleavage between the politics of particularistic identity and the politics of cosmopolitan or hu-manist values.

The Characteristics of Globalization

In his book *Nations and Nationalism* Ernest Gellner analyses the association between nationalism and industrialization.[1] He de-scribes the emergence of vertically organized secular national cultures based on vernacular languages which enabled people to cope with the demands of modernity – everyday encounters with industry and government. As varied rural occupations were replaced with factory production and as the state intruded into more and more aspects of daily life, people needed to be able to communicate both verbally and in writing in a common administrative language, and they needed to acquire certain standardized skills. Earlier societies were characterized by horizontal high cultures, e.g. Latin, Persian, Sanskrit, etc., which were based on religion and were not necessarily linked to the state. These were combined with a great variety of vertical low folk cultures. Whereas earlier high cultures were reproduced in religious institutions and low cultures were passed on through oral traditions, the new vertical national cultures were generated by a new class of intellectuals – writers, journalists, schoolteachers – which emerged along with the establishment of printing, the publication of secular literature such as newspapers and novels, and the expansion of primary education.

The process of globalization, it can be argued, has begun to break up these vertically organized cultures. What appear to be emerging are new horizontal cultures arising out of the new transnational networks, often based on the use of the English language, including the culture of mass consumerism associated with globally known names such as Coca Cola or McDonald's, combined with a medley of national, local and regional cultures as a result of a new assertion of local particularities.

The term globalization conceals a complex process which actually involves both globalization and localization, integration and fragmentation, homogenization and differentiation, etc. On the one hand, the process creates inclusive transnational networks of people. On the other hand, it excludes and atomises large numbers of people – indeed, the vast majority. On the one hand, people's lives are profoundly shaped by events taking place far away from where they live over which they have no control. On the other hand, there are new possibilities for enhancing the role of local and regional politics through being linked in to global processes.

As a process, globalization has a long history. Indeed, some argue that there is nothing new about the present phase of globalization; from its inception, capitalism was always a global phenomenon.[2] What is new, however, in the last two decades, is the astonishing revolution in information and communications technology. I would argue that these technological changes impart a qualitative deepening to the process of globalization which is, as yet, by no means determined. The current contours of the process are shaped by the post-war institutional framework and, in particular, the deregulatory policies pursued by governments during the 1980s. Its future will depend on the evolution of political and social values, actions and forms of organization. Here, I outline some key trends relevant to an understanding of that evolution.

In the economic sphere, globalization is associated with a set of changes variously described as post-Fordism, flexible specialization, fujitsuism. These changes generally refer to a change in what is known as the technico-economic paradigm, the prevailing way in which supply of products and services is organized to meet the prevailing pattern of demand.[3] The relevant features of these changes are the dramatic decline in the importance of territorially-based mass production, the globalization of finance and technology and the increased specialization and diversity of markets. Improved information means that physical production is less important as a share of the overall economy, both because of the increased importance of services and because an increasing proportion of the value of individual products consists of know-how – design, marketing, legal and financial advice. Likewise, the standardization of products, which is linked to territorially-based economies of scale, can be supplanted by greater differentiation according to local or specialist demand. Hence, national levels of economic organization have declined in importance along with the decreased emphasis on territorially-based production. On the other hand, global levels of economic organization have greatly expanded because of the global character of finance and technology, while local levels of economic organization have also become more significant because of the increasing differentiation of markets.

Globalization also involves the transnationalization and regionalization of governance. There has been, since the war, an explosive growth in international organizations, regimes and regulatory agencies. More and more activities of government are regulated through international agreement or integrated into transnational institutions; more and more departments and ministries are engaged in formal and informal forms of cooperation with their equivalents in other countries; more and more policy decisions are co-opted upwards to often unaccountable international fora. At the same time, the last two decades have witnessed a reassertion of local and regional politics especially, but not only, for development purposes. This reassertion has taken a variety of forms ranging from science- and business-led initiatives, as in the case of 'technopoles' like Silicon Valley or Cambridge, England; a rediscovery of municipal traditions, as in Northern Italy; peace- or Green-led initiatives such as nuclear-free zones or waste-recycling projects; as well as new or renewed forms of local clientelism and patronage.[4]

Parallel to the changing nature of governance has been a striking growth in informal non-governmental transnational networks.[5] These include NGOs – both those which undertake functions formerly undertaken by government, e.g. humanitarian assistance, and those which campaign on global issues, e.g. human rights, ecology, peace, etc.[5] These NGOs are most active at local and transnational levels, partly because these are the sites of the problems with which they are concerned and partly because access to national politics is blocked by nationally organized political parties. Thus, organizations like Greenpeace or Amnesty International are known all over the world; yet their influence on national governments is limited. In addition, other kinds of transnational network have flourished: links between a variety of cultural and sporting activities; transnational religious and ethnic groups; transnational crime. Tertiary education is increasingly globalized both because of student and faculty exchanges, and because of the privileged use of the internet.

These economic and political changes also involve far-reaching changes in organizational forms. Most societies are characterized by what Bukharin called a 'monism of architecture'.[6] In the modern era, nation-states, enterprises and military organizations had very similar vertical forms of hierarchical organization – the influence of modern war, particularly the experience of the Second World War on organizational forms, was pervasive. Robert Reich, in his book *The Work of Nations*, describes how enterprises have been transformed from national vertical organizations, where power is concentrated in the hands of owners at the top of a pyramid-shaped chain of command, into global phenomena whose organizations most resemble a spider's web, with power in the hands of those who possess technical or financial know-how and who are spread around the points of the web:

> Their dignified headquarters, expansive factories, warehouses, laboratories, and fleets of trucks and corporate jets are leased. Their production workers, janitors, and bookkeepers are under temporary contract; their key researchers, design engineers and marketeers are sharing in the profits. And their distinguished executives, rather than possessing great power and authority over this domain, have little direct control over much of anything. Instead of imposing their will over a corporate empire, they guide ideas through the new webs of enterprise.[7]

Something similar is happening to governmental and non-governmental organizations. Government departments, at all levels, are developing horizontal transnational links; government activity is increasingly contracted out through various forms of privatization and semi-privatization arrangements. The decentralized and horizontal forms of organization typical of NGOs or new social movements are often contrasted to the traditional, vertical forms of organization typical of political parties.[8] Political leaders, like corporate executives, are, at most, facilitators and opinion-shapers and, at least, images or symbols – public representations of interconnected webs of activity over which they have little control.

Globalization has profoundly affected social structures. In advanced industrial countries, the traditional working classes have declined or are declining along with the drop in territorially-based mass production. Because of improvements in productivity and because production work is less skilled, manufacturing production employs fewer and lower-paid workers, especially women and immigrants, or else it is relocated to low-wage countries.

What has grown has been those people whom Alain Touraine calls information workers[9] and Robert Reich calls symbolic analysts, those people who possess and use know-how, who, to quote Reich, identify, solve and broker problems through 'manipulations of symbols – data, words, oral and visual representations'.[10] These are the people who work in technology or finance, in expanded higher education, or in the growing myriad of transnational organizations. The majority of people fit neither of these two categories. They either work in services, as waiters and waitresses, salespersons, taxi-drivers, cashiers, etc., or they join the growing ranks of unemployed made redundant by the productivity increases associated with globalization. This emerging social structure is reflected in growing income disparities both between those in work and those not in work and among those in work depending on skill.

Income disparities are also associated with geographical disparities, both within and across continents, countries and regions. There is the growing disparity between those areas, mainly the advanced industrial regions, that can capitalize on their technological capabilities and the rest. Some areas may thrive, at least temporarily, through attracting volume production, i.e. Southeast Asia, Southern Europe and, potentially, Central Europe. The remainder are caught up in the global economy as traditional sources of livelihood are eroded but can participate neither in production nor consumption. Maps drawn by global enterprises of the segmentation of their markets generally leave out the larger part of the world. But even within countries, continents or even cities, these widening geographical disparities can be found – and this is true of both the advanced industrial world and the rest. Everywhere, boundaries are being drawn between protected and prosperous global enclaves and the anarchic chaotic poverty-stricken areas beyond.

The trends outlined above are simultaneously haphazard and constructed. There is no inevitability, for example, about the growth of social, economic and geographical disparities; in part, they are the consequence of disorganization or of organization evolving out of past inertia. What can, however, be accepted as a given is the historic shift away from vertical cultures characteristic of the era of the nation-state which gave rise to a sense of national identity and a sense of security. The abstract symbols, like money and law, which form the basis of social relations in societies no longer dominated by face-to-face interactions, were a constitutive part of these national cultures.[11] It is now commonplace to talk about a 'crisis of identity' – a sense of alienation and disorientation that accompanies the decomposition of cultural communities.

It is also possible, however, to point to certain emerging forms of cultural classification. On the one hand, there are those who see themselves as part of a global community of like-minded people, mainly well-educated information workers or symbolic analysts, who spend a lot of time on aeroplanes, tele-conferencing, etc., and who may work for a global corporation, an NGO, or some other international organization or who may be part of a network of scholars or sports clubs or musicians and artists, etc. On the other hand, there are those who are excluded and who may or may not see themselves as part of a local or particularistic (religious or national) community.

As yet, the emerging global groupings are not politicized, or, at least, are hardly politicized. That is to say they do not form the basis of political communities on which new forms of power could be based. One reason is the individualism and anomie that characterizes the current period: the sense that political action is futile given the enormity of current problems, the difficulty of controlling or influencing the web-like structure of power, the cultural fragmentation both of horizontal networks and particularistic loyalties. Both what Reich calls the laisser-faire cosmopolitan who has 'seceded' from the nation-state and who pursues his or her individualistic consumerist interests, and the restless young criminals, the new adventurers, to be found in all the excluded zones, reflect this political vacuum.

Nevertheless, there are seeds of politicization in both group-ings. Cosmopolitan politicization can be located both within the new transnational NGOs or social movements and within inter-national institutions, as well as among individuals, around a com-mitment to human values (universal social and political rights, ecological responsibility, peace and democracy, etc.) and to the notion of transnational civil society – the idea that self-organized groups, operating across borders, can solve problems and lobby political institutions. The new politics of particularistic identities can also be interpreted as a response to these global processes, as a form of political mobilization in the face of the growing impotence of the modern state.

Identity Politics

I use the term 'identity politics' to mean movements which mobilize around ethnic, racial or religious identity for the pur-pose of claiming state power.[12] And I use the term 'identity' narrowly to mean a form of labelling. Whether we are talking about tribal conflict in Africa, religious conflict in the Middle

East or South Asia, or nationalist conflict in Europe, the common feature is the way in which labels are used as a basis for political claims. Such conflicts are often described as ethnic conflicts. The term ethnos has a racial connotation even though a number of writers insist that 'ethnie' refers to a cultural community rather than a blood-based community. Although it is clear that there is no racial basis to ethnic claims, the point is that these labels tend to be treated as something you are born with and cannot change; they cannot be acquired through conversion or assimilation. You are German if your grandmother was German, even if you cannot speak the language and have never been to Germany; but you are not German if your parents were Turkish, even if you live and work in Germany. A Catholic born in West Belfast is doomed to remain a Catholic even if he or she converts to Protestantism. A Croat cannot become a Serb by adopting the Orthodox religion and writing in a Cyrillic script. To the extent that these labels are considered birthrights, conflicts based on identity politics can also be termed ethnic conflicts. There are, of course, forms of identity politics where labels are not birthrights but can be voluntarily or forcibly imposed. Certain sects of militant Islam, for example, aim to create pure Islamic states through the conversion of non-Muslims.[13]

The term 'politics' refers to the claim to state power. In many parts of the world, there are religious revivals, or renewed interest in the survival of local cultures and languages and this, in part, is a response to the stresses of globalization. Political campaigns to protect or promote religion or culture may often lead to demands for power. Nevertheless, this is not what is meant by identity politics. Such political campaigns are demands for cultural and religious rights. These are quite different from the demand for political rights based on identity. The latter is a form of communitarianism that is distinct from and may conflict with individual political rights.

The politics of identity can be contrasted with the politics of ideas. The politics of ideas is about forward-looking projects. Thus, religious struggles in Western Europe in the seventeenth century were about freeing the individual from the oppressive hold of the established Church. Early nationalist struggles in nineteenth-century Europe or colonial Africa were about democracy and state-building. They were conceived as ways of welding together diverse groups of people under the rubric of nation for the purpose of modernization. More recently, politics has been dominated by abstract secular ideas like socialism or environmentalism which offer a vision for the future. This type of politics tends to be integrative, embracing all those who support the idea, even though, as recent experience has demonstrated, the universalistic character of such ideas can serve as a justification for totalitarian and authoritarian practices.

In contrast, identity politics tends to be fragmentative, backward-looking and exclusive. Political groupings based on exclusive identity tend to be movements of nostalgia, based on the reconstruction of an heroic past, the memory of injustices, real or imagined, and of famous battles, won or lost. They acquire meaning through insecurity, through rekindled fear of historic enemies, or through a sense of being threatened by those with different labels. Labels can always be divided and sub-divided. There is no such thing as cultural purity or homogeneity. Every exclusive identity-based polity necessarily generates a minority. At best, identity politics involves psychological discrimination against those labelled differently. At worst, it leads to population expulsion and genocide.

The new identity politics arises out of the disintegration or erosion of modern state structures, especially centralized, authoritarian states. The collapse of communist states after 1989, the loss of legitimacy of post-colonial states in Africa or South Asia, or even the decline of welfare states in more advanced industrial countries provide the environment in which the new forms of identity politics are nurtured.

The new identity politics has two main sources, both of which are linked to globalization. On the one hand, it can be viewed as a reaction to the growing impotence and declining legitimacy of the established political classes. From this perspective, it is a politics fostered from above which plays to and inculcates popular prejudices. It is a form of political mobilization, a survival tactic, for politicians active in national politics either at the level of the state or at the level of nationally defined regions, as in the case of the republics of the former Yugoslavia or the former Soviet Union or in places like Kashmir or Eritrea before independence. On the other hand, it emerges out of what can be described as the parallel economy – new forms of legal and illegal ways of making a living that have sprung up among the excluded parts of society – and constitutes a way of legitimizing these new shadowy forms of activity. Particularly in Eastern Europe, the events of 1989 compressed the impact of globalization both in under-mining the nation-state and in releasing new forms of economic activity into a short 'transitional' space of time, so that this form of nationalism from below combined with nationalism from above in an explosive combination.[14]

In Eastern Europe, the use of nationalism as a form of politi-cal mobilization pre-dated 1989. Particularly in the former com-munist multinational states, national consciousness was deliberately cultivated in a context in which ideological differ-ences had been disallowed and when societies had, in theory, been socially homogenized and 'socially cleansed'.[15] National-ity, or certain officially recognized nationalities, became the main legitimate umbrella for pursuing various forms of political, eco-nomic and cultural interests. This was particularly important in the former Yugoslavia and Soviet Union, where national differ-ence was 'constitutionally enshrined'.[16]

These tendencies were reinforced by the functioning of econo-mies of shortage. In theory, planned economies are supposed to eliminate competition. Such planning does of course eliminate competition for markets. But it gives rise to another form of competition – competition for resources. In theory, the plan is drawn up by rational planners and transmitted downwards through a vertical chain of command. In practice, the plan is 'built up' through a myriad of bureaucratic pressures and subse-quently 'broken down'. In effect, the plan operates as an expres-sion of bureaucratic compromise and, because of the 'soft budget' constraint, individual enterprises always spend more than is planned. The consequence is a vicious circle in which shortage intensifies the competition for resources and the tendency among ministries and enterprises for hoarding and autarky which fur-ther intensifies shortage. In this context, nationality becomes a tool which can be used to further the competition for resources.[17]

Already, in the early 1970s there were writers who were warning of a nationalist explosion in the former Soviet Union as a result of the way in which nationality policy was used to prop up the decaying socialist project.[18] In a classic article, published in 1974, Teresa Rakowska-Harmstone used the term the 'new nationalism' to describe 'a new phenomenon which is present even among people who, at the time of the revolution, had only an inchoate sense of a common culture'.[19] Soviet policy created a hierarchy of nationalities based on an elaborate administrative hierarchy in which the status of nationalities was linked to the status of territorially-based administrative units – republic, autonomous regions and autonomous areas. Within these administrative arrangements, the indigenous language and culture of the so-called 'titular' nationality was promoted and members of the titular nationality were given priority in local administration and education.[20] The system gave rise to what Zaslavsky has described as an 'explosive division of labour' in which an indigenous administrative and intellectual elite presided over an imported Russian urban working class and an indigenous rural population.[21] The local elite used the development of national consciousness to promote administrative autonomy, especially in the economic sphere.

As I argued in the previous chapter, a similar process took place in the former Yugoslavia especially after the 1974 constitution entrenched the nations and republics that made up the federation and restricted the powers of the federal government. What held these multinational states together was the monopoly of the Communist Party. In the aftermath of 1989, when the socialist project was discredited and the monopoly of the party was finally broken and when democratic elections were held for the first time, nationalism erupted into the open. In a situation where there is little to choose between parties, where there has been no history of political debate, where the new politicians are hardly known, nationalism becomes a mechanism for political differentiation. In societies where people assume that they are expected to vote in certain ways, where they are not habituated to political choice and may be wary of taking it for granted, voting along national lines became the most obvious option.

Nationalism represents both a continuity with the past and a way of denying or 'forgetting' a complicity with the past. It represents a continuity partly because of the ways in which it was nurtured in the preceding era not only in multinational states and partly because its form is very similar to the preceding Cold War ideologies. Communism, in particular, thrived on a we–they, good–bad, war mentality and elevated the notion of an homogeneous collective community. At the same time, it is a way of denying the past because communist regimes overtly condemned nationalism. As in the case of rabid attachment to the market, nationalism is a form of negation of what went before. Communism can be treated as an 'outsider' or 'foreigner', particularly in countries occupied by Soviet troops, thus exculpating those who accepted, tolerated or collaborated with the regime. National identity is somehow pure and untainted in comparison with other professional or ideological identities that were determined by the previous context.

Some similar, although less extreme tendencies, can be observed in other places. Already, by the 1970s and 1980s the fragility of post-colonial administrative structures was becoming apparent. States in Africa and Asia were having to cope with the disillusion of post-independence hopes, the failure of the development project to overcome poverty and inequality, the insecurity of rapid urbanization and the break-up of traditional rural communities, as well as the impact of structural adjustment and policies of stabilization, liberalization and deregularization. Moreover, as in the case of ex-Yugoslavia, the loss of an international identity based on membership of the non-aligned movement in the aftermath of the Cold War had domestic repercussions as well. Both ruling politicians and aspiring opposition leaders began to play upon particularistic identities in different ways – to justify authoritarian policies, to create scapegoats, to mobilize support around fear and insecurity. In many post-colonial states, the ruling parties saw themselves as left parties occupying the space for emancipatory movements. As in post-communist states, the absence of a legitimate emancipatory movement opened politics up to claims based on tribe or clan, or religious or linguistic group.

In the pre-colonial period, most societies had only a loose sense of ethnic identity. The Europeans, with their passion for classification, with censuses and identity papers, imposed more rigid ethnic categories, which then evolved along with the growth of communication, roads and railways, and the emergence, in some countries, of a vernacular press. In some cases, the categories were quite artificial: the Hutu–Tutsi distinction in Rwanda and Burundi was a rough, largely social distinction before the Belgian administration introduced identity cards; likewise, the Ngala, the tribe President Mobutu of Zaire claimed to come from, was largely a Belgian invention. In the post-independence period, most ruling parties espoused a secular national identity that embraced the often numerous ethnic groups within the artificially defined territory of the new nations. As post-independence hopes faded, many politicians began to appeal to particularistic tendencies. In general, the weaker the administrative structures the earlier this took place. In some countries, like Sudan, Nigeria or Zaire, what have been called 'predatory' regimes developed in which access to power and personal wealth depended on religion or tribe.[22] In India, where democracy was sustained for almost all of the post-independence period, the Congress Party's use of Hindu rituals and symbols in the 1970s paved the way for new forms of political mobilization based on identity, particularly religion.[23]

Many of these states were strongly interventionist. As foreign assistance began to be replaced by commercial borrowing in the 1970s, as foreign debt mounted and 'structural adjustment' programmes were introduced, state revenues declined and, as in the former communist countries, political competition for control over resources intensified. The end of the Cold War meant the reduction of foreign assistance to countries like Zaire or Somalia which had been considered strategically important. At the same time, pressure for democratization led to increasingly desperate bids to remain in power, often through fomenting ethnic tension.

Even in Western Europe, the erosion of legitimacy associated with the declining autonomy of the nation-state and the corrosion of traditional, often industrially-based sources of social cohesion became much more transparent in the aftermath of 1989. It was no longer possible to defend democracy with reference to its absence elsewhere. A specifically Western identity defined in relation to the Soviet threat was undermined. And the distinctive character of national identity defined in relation to the Cold War lost its substance; for example Gaullism in France, the British special relationship with the United States, or the Greek role as East–West broker in the Balkans. Germany is, of course, a special case, gaining a new national identity in the ruins of the Berlin Wall and making possible the rediscovery of buried history.

Of equal significance is the political vacuum, the decline of the left and the narrowing space for substantive political difference. Nationalism, or seeds of nationalism like asylum laws, are exploited as party political forms of differentiation. The left offers no clear opposition or worse, particularly those parts of the left discredited by the fall of communism. In France, Jean-Marie

Le Pen, leader of the Front National, draws support from former communist voters. The Panhellenic Socialist Movement (PASOK) in Greece plays the nationalist card.[24]

Western countries do not of course share the experience of collectivist authoritarianism, although regions like Northern Ireland where particularist politics are strong tend to be those where democracy has been weak. An active civil society tends to counterbalance the distrust of politicians, the alienation from political institutions, the sense of apathy and futility that provide a potential basis for populist tendencies. Nevertheless, the 'secession' of the new cosmopolitan classes and the fragmentation and dependence of those excluded from the benefits of globalization are characteristic of advanced industrial countries as well.

The other main source of the new identity politics is the parallel economy. This is, to a large extent, the product of neo-liberal policies pursued in the 1980s and the 1990s – macro-economic stabilization, deregulation and privatization – which effectively represented a speeding up of the process of globalization. These policies increased the level of unemployment, resource depletion and disparities in income which provided an environment for growing criminalization and the creation of networks of corruption, black marketeers, arms and drug traffickers, etc. In societies where the state controlled large parts of the economy and where self-organized market institutions do not exist, policies of 'structural adjustment' or 'transition' effectively mean the absence of any kind of regulation. The market does not, by and large, mean new autonomous productive enterprises. It means corruption, speculation and crime. New groups of shady 'businessmen', often linked in to the decaying institutional apparatuses through various forms of bribery and 'insider' dealing, are engaged in a kind of primitive accumulation – a grab for land and capital. They use the language of identity politics to build alliances and to legitimize their activities. Often these networks are linked to wars, e.g. in Afghanistan, Pakistan and large parts of Africa, and to the disintegration of the military-industrial complex in the aftermath of the Cold War. Often, they are transnational, linking up to international circuits of illegal goods sometimes through diaspora connections.

A typical phenomenon is the new bands of young men, the new adventurers, who make a living through violence or through threats of violence, who obtain surplus weapons through the black market or through looting military stores, and who either base their power on particularistic networks or who seek respectability through particularistic claims. They also include hostage-takers in the Transcaucasus who capture hostages in order to exchange them for food, weapons, money, other hostages and even dead bodies; mafia-rings in Russia; the new Cossacks who don the Cossack uniform in order to 'protect' Russian diaspora groups in the near abroad; nationalist militia groups of unemployed youths in Western Ukraine or Western Herzegovina – all feed, like vultures, on the remnants of the disintegrating state and on the frustrations and resentments of the poor and unemployed. A similar breed of restless political adventurer is to be found in conflict areas in Africa and South Asia.[25]

The new identity politics combines these two sources of particularism in varying degrees. Former administrative or intellectual elites ally with a motley collection of adventurers on the margins of society to mobilize the excluded and abandoned, alienated and insecure for the purposes of capturing and sustaining power. The greater the sense of insecurity, the greater the polarization of society, the less is the space for alternative integrative political values. In conditions of war, such alliances are cemented by shared complicity in war crimes and a mutual dependence on the continued functioning of the war economy. In Rwanda, the plan for mass genocide has been explained as the way in which the extremist Hutus could retain their grip on power in the context of economic crisis and international pressure for democratization. According to the NGO Africa Rights: 'The extremists' aim was for the entire Hutu populace to participate in the killings. That way, the blood of genocide would stain everybody. There could be no going back.'[26] The intensification of the war in Kashmir, including the involvement of Afghan *Mujahidiin* has created a polarization between Hindu and Muslim identities which has increasingly supplanted syncretic traditions and the common bonds based on Kashmiri identity – the *kashmiriyat*.[27] One of the explanations for the ferocity of nationalist sentiment in the former Yugoslavia is the fact that all the various sources of the new identity politics are concentrated there: the former Yugoslavia had the most Westernized, indeed cosmopolitan, elite of any East European country, thus exacerbating the resentments of those excluded; it experienced nationalistic bureaucratic competition typical of the centralized state in decline; and because it was exposed to the transition to the market earlier than other East European countries, its parallel economy was more developed. Even so, a vicious war was required to create the hatred on which exclusive identities could be reconstructed.

The new form of identity politics is often treated as a throw-back to the past, a return to pre-modern identities temporarily displaced or suppressed by modernizing ideologies. It is of course the case that the new politics draws on memory and history and that certain societies where cultural traditions are more entrenched are more susceptible to the new politics. But, as I have argued, what really matters is the recent past and, in particular, the im-pact of globalization on the political survival of states. Moreover, the new politics has entirely new contemporary attributes.

First of all, it is horizontal as well as vertical, transnational as well as national. In nearly all the new nationalisms, the diaspora play a much more important role than formerly because of the speed of communication. There were always expatriate national-ist groups plotting their country's liberation in cafés in Paris or London. But such groups have become much larger and more sig-nificant because of the scale of emigration, the ease of travel and the spread of telephones, faxes and electronic mail. There are two types of diaspora. On the one hand, there are minorities living in the near abroad, fearful of their vulnerability to local nationalisms and often more extreme than those living on home territory. These include Serbians living in Croatia and Bosnia–Herzegovina, Rus-sian minorities in all the new ex-Soviet republics, the Hungarian minority in Vojvodina, Romania, Ukraine and Slovakia, Tutsis liv-ing in Zaire or Uganda. On the other hand, there are disaffected groups living far away, often in the new melting-pot nations, who find solace in fantasies about their origins which are often far re-moved from reality. The idea of a Sikh homeland, Khalistan, the notion of uniting Macedonia and Bulgaria, the call for an inde-pendent Ruthenia – all originated from diaspora communities in Canada. Irish-American support for the Irish Republican Army (IRA), violent conflict between the Greek and Macedonian com-munities in Australia and the pressure from Croatian groups in Germany for recognition of Croatia are all further examples. These groups provide ideas, money, arms and know-how, often with dis-proportionate effects. Among the individuals who make up the new nationalist compacts are romantic expatriates, foreign mer-cenaries, dealers and investors, Canadian pizza-parlour owners, etc. Radha Kumar has described the support given by Indians living in the United States to Hindu fundamentalists: 'Separated from their countries of origin, often living as aliens in a foreign land, simultaneously feeling stripped of their culture and guilty for having escaped the troubles 'back home', expatriates turn to diaspora nationalism without understanding the violence that their actions might inadvertently trigger.'[28] The same kind of transnational networks are to be found among religious groupings. Islamic connections are well known, but such links also apply to other religious groupings. I visited the office of the so-called foreign minister of South Ossetia, a breakaway region of Georgia, and he had a picture of the Bosnian Serb leader, Karadžić, on his wall. He explained that he had been given it by the delegation from Republika Srbska when he attended a meeting of Eastern Orthodox Christians.

Second, the capacity for political mobilization is greatly extended both as a result of the improved education and the expansion of educated classes and as a consequence of new technologies. Many explanations for the growth of political Islam focus on the emergence of newly literate urban classes, who are often excluded from power, the increase in Islamic schools and the expansion of newspaper readership.[29] Growing literacy in the vernacular languages, together with the spread of tabloid-type communitarian newspapers, creates new 'imagined communities'. Even more significantly, the widespread availability of television, videos and radio offers extremely rapid and effective ways of disseminating a particularistic message. The electronic media has an authority that newspapers cannot match; in parts of Africa, the radio is 'magic'. The circulation of cassettes with sermons by militant Islamic preachers, the use of 'hate' radio to incite people to genocide in Rwanda, the control of television by nationalist leaders in Eastern Europe – all provide mechanisms for speeding up the pace of political mobilization. In Kosovo, diaspora and modern communications come together in Albanian language broadcasts from Switzerland received by the Albanian population through their satellite dishes.

Cosmopolitanism versus Particularism

A. D. Smith, in his book *Nations and Nationalism in the Global Era*, takes issue with the view that nation-states are an anachronism.[30] He argues that the new global classes still need to feel a sense of community and identity based on ethnies to overcome the alienation of their technical scientific universalizing discourse. And he criticizes what he calls the modernist fallacy that nation-states are artificial and temporary polities, staging-posts in the evolution towards global society. He sees the new nationalism as evidence of the persistence of ethnies and he offers a positive perspective on cultural separatism which he sees as a way of grounding nation-states more firmly round a dominant ethnie, while, at the same time, enabling them to embrace civic ideals.

It may well be that the new particularistic identities are here to stay, that they are the expression of a new post-modern cultural relativism. But it is difficult to argue that they offer a basis for humanistic civic values precisely because they are unable to offer a forward-looking project relevant to the new global context. The main implication of globalization is that territorial sovereignty is no longer viable. The effort to reclaim power within a particular spatial domain will merely further undermine the ability to influence events. This does not mean that the new form of particularistic identity politics will go away. Rather, it is a recipe for new closed-in chaotic statelets with permanently contested borders dependent on continuing violence for survival.

The particularists cannot do without those people who are labelled differently. Globalization, as its name implies, is global. Everywhere, in varying proportions, those who benefit from globalization have to share territory with those excluded from its benefits who are nevertheless deeply affected by it. Both losers and gainers need each other. No patch of territory, however small or large, can any longer insulate itself from the outside world.

Of course, it is possible to envisage, and it is already happening, a new assertion of regional and local politics, a claim for greater democratic accountability at regional and local levels. But such claims would have to be situated in a global context; they would have to involve greater access and openness towards global levels of governance and they would have to be based on greater democratic accountability for all inhabitants of the territory in question, not just for those with a particular label. This type of politics would thus need to be embedded in what might be described as a cosmopolitan political consciousness.

By cosmopolitanism, I do not mean a denial of identity. Rather,

I mean a celebration of the diversity of global identities, acceptance and, indeed, enthusiasm for multiple overlapping identities, and, at the same time, a commitment to the equality of all
human beings and to respect for human dignity. The term origi-
nates in the Kantian notion of cosmopolitan right that is combined with recognition of separate sovereignties; thus it brings
together both universalism and diversity. Anthony Appiah talks
about the 'cosmopolitan patriot' or the 'rooted cosmopolitan,
attached to a home of one's own, with its own cultural particularities, but taking pleasure from the presence of other different
people'. He distinguishes cosmopolitanism from humanism 'because cosmopolitanism is not just the feeling that everybody
matters. For the cosmopolitan also celebrates the fact that there
are *different* local human ways of being; humanism, by contrast,
is consistent with the desire for global homogeneity.'[31]

Two possible sources of a cosmopolitan political consciousness can be identified. One, which could be described as
cosmopolitanism from above, is to be found in the growing
myriad of international organizations, a few of which, most notably the EU, are developing supra-national powers. These institutions develop their own logics and internal structures. They
enable activities to be carried out rather than undertaking them
through their own resources. They function through complex
partnerships, cooperation agreements, negotiation and mediation with other organizations, states, and private or semi-private
groups. They are restricted both by lack of resources and,
relatedly, by the inter-governmental arrangements which make
it extremely difficult for them to act, except on the basis of time-
consuming and often unsatisfactory compromises. In many of
these institutions there are committed idealistic officials. They
have an interest in seeking alternative sources of legitimacy to
their frustrating national masters.

The other source is what could be described as cosmopolitanism from below, the new social movements of the 1980s
and what have come to be called NGOs in the 1990s. This new
form of activism has developed since the early 1980s primarily
in response to new global problems. These movements differ
from earlier social movements. They do not easily fit a traditional left–right divide; they are concerned with new issues –
peace, ecology, human rights, gender, development. They tend
to be horizontal rather than vertical in organization, operating

most effectively at local and transnational levels. In the 1990s, they have increasingly functioned in individualistic ways. They tend to be sceptical about politics. They express their individual commitments through vegetarianism or through driving convoys of aid to war zones. Although they have in the past organized mass demonstrations, their actions tend to be symbolic or spectacular – as, for example, the activities of the Greenpeace ship *Rainbow Warrior*. Terms like 'anti-politics', 'self-organization' and 'civil society' express their disaffection with conventional political forms.

At present, cosmopolitanism and particularism coexist side by side in the same geographical space. Cosmopolitanism tends to be more widespread in the West and less widespread in the East and South. Nevertheless, throughout the world, in remote villages and towns, both sorts of people are to be found. The new particularistic conflicts throw up courageous groups of people who try to oppose war and exclusivism – both local people and those who volunteer to come from abroad to provide humanitarian assistance, to help mediate, etc. Local groups gather strength in so far as they can gain access to or support and protection from transnational networks.

It is in wars that the space for cosmopolitanism is narrowed. Particularisms need each other to sustain their exclusive identities; hence the paradoxical combination of conflict and cooperation. It is cosmopolitanism that undermines the appeal of particularism and it is the representatives of humane civic values that are often targeted in wars. More and more no-go areas come into being, like Rwanda or Afghanistan where isolated humanitarian agencies gingerly negotiate and bribe their way through to help those in need. Some argue that such situations are the harbingers of the future for much of the world.[32] Nothing is more polarizing than violence and more likely to induce a retreat from utopian inclusive projects. 'Sarajevo is Europe's future. This is the end of history', Sarajevo's disenchanted cosmopolitans will tell you. But politics is never determined. Whether another future can be envisaged is, in the end, a matter of choice.

5

The Globalized War Economy

The term 'war economy' usually refers to a system which is centralized, totalizing and autarchic, as was the case in the total wars of the twentieth century. Administration is centralized to increase the efficiency of the war and to maximize revenue to pay for the war. As many people as possible are mobilized to participate in the war effort either as soldiers or in the production of arms and necessities. By and large, the war effort is self-sufficient, although in World War II, Britain and the Soviet Union received lend-lease assistance from the United States. The main aim of the war effort is to maximize the use of force so as to engage and defeat the enemy in battle.

The new type of war economy is almost totally the opposite. The new wars are 'globalized' wars. They involve the fragmentation and decentralization of the state. Participation is low relative to the population both because of lack of pay and because of lack of legitimacy on the part of the warring parties. There is very little domestic production, so the war effort is heavily dependent on local predation and external support. Battles are rare, most violence is directed against civilians, and cooperation between warring factions is common.

Those who conceive of war in traditional Clausewitzean terms, based on definable geo-political goals, fail to understand the underlying vested interests, both political and economic, in the continuation of war. They tend to assume that political solutions can be found without any need to address the underlying economic logic. At the same time, however, those who recognize the irrelevance of traditional perceptions of war and observe the complexity of the political, social and economic relationships expressed in these wars tend to conclude that this type of violence can be equated with anarchy. In these circumstances, the most that can be done is to treat the symptoms through, for example, humanitarian assistance.

In this chapter, I argue that it is possible to analyse the typical political economy of new wars so as to draw conclusions about possible alternative approaches. Indeed, the implication of such an analysis is that many of the well-meaning efforts of various international actors, based on inherited assumptions about the character of war, may turn out to be counterproductive. Conflict resolution from above may merely enhance the legitimacy of the warring parties and allow time for replenishment; humanitarian assistance may contribute to the functioning of the war economy; peacekeeping troops may lose legitimacy either by standing aside when terrible crimes are committed or by siding with groups who commit terrible crimes.

In the first section, I describe the various fighting units typical of contemporary wars and how they have emerged out of the disintegration of the state's formal security capacities. Then, I analyse patterns of violence and the character of military strategy and the way these have evolved out of the conflicts that developed during and after the Second World War as a way of reacting against or coping with modern conventional war – guerrilla warfare, counterinsurgency, and the 'low-intensity' conflicts of the 1980s. Next, I consider how the fighting units acquire resources with which to fight the new wars and the interaction between the new pattern of violence and the social relations that are generated in the context of war. In the final section, I describe how the new wars, or rather the social conditions of the new wars, tend to spread.

The Privatization of Military Forces

Madeleine Albright, the US Secretary of State, has used the term 'failed states' to describe countries with weak or non-existent central authority – the classic examples are Somalia or Afghanistan. Jeffrey Herbst argues that many African states never enjoyed state sovereignty in the modern sense – that is, 'unquestioned physical control over the defined territory, but also an administrative presence throughout the country and the allegiance of the population to the idea of the state'.[1] One of the key characteristics of failing states is the loss of control over and fragmentation of the instruments of physical coercion. A disintegrative cycle sets in which is almost the exact opposite of the integrative cycle through which modern states were established. The failure to sustain physical control over the territory and to command popular allegiance reduces the ability to collect taxes and greatly weakens the revenue base of the state. In addition, corruption and personalistic rule represents an added drain on state revenue. Often, the government can no longer afford reliable forms of tax collection; private agencies are sometimes employed who keep part of the takings, much as happened in Europe in the eighteenth century. Tax evasion is widespread both because of the loss of state legitimacy and because of the emergence of new forces who claim 'protection money'. This leads to outside pressure to cut government spending, which further reduces the capacity to maintain control and encourages the fragmentation of military units. Moreover, outside assistance is predicated on economic and political reforms which many of these states are constitutionally incapable of implementing. A downward spiral of loss of revenue and legitimacy, growing disorder and military fragmentation creates the context in which the new wars take place. Effectively, the 'failure' of the state is accompanied by a growing privatization of violence.

Typically, the new wars are characterized by a multiplicity of types of fighting units both public and private, state and non-state, or some kind of mixture. For the purpose of simplicity, I identify five main types: regular armed forces or remnants thereof; paramilitary groups; self-defence units; foreign mercenaries; and, finally, regular foreign troops generally under international auspices.

Regular armed forces are in decay, particularly in areas of conflict. Cuts in military spending, declining prestige, shortages of equipment, spare parts, fuel and ammunition, and inadequate training all contribute to a profound loss of morale. In many African and post-Soviet states, soldiers no longer receive training or regular pay. They may have to seek out their own sources of funding which contributes to indiscipline and breakdown of the military hierarchy. Often this leads to fragmentation, situations in which local army commanders act as local warlords, as in Tadjikistan. Or soldiers may engage in criminal behaviour as, for example, in Zaire, where unpaid soldiers were encouraged to loot or pillage. In other words, regular armed forces lose their character as the legitimate bearer of arms and become increasingly difficult to distinguish from private paramilitary groups. This is compounded in situations where the security forces were already fragmented as a result of deliberate policy; often there were border guards, a presidential guard, a gendarmerie, not to mention various types of internal security forces. By the end, President Mobutu of Zaire could rely only on his personal guard to protect him.

The most common fighting units are paramilitary groups, that is to say, autonomous groups of armed men generally centred around an individual leader. Often these groups are established by governments in order to distance themselves from the more extreme manifestations of violence. This was probably the case for Arkan's Tigers in Bosnia, or so Arkan himself insisted. Likewise, the pre–1994 Rwandan government recruited unemployed young men to a newly formed militia linked to the ruling party; they were given training by the Rwandan army and a small salary.[2] In a similar vein, the South African government secretly supplied arms and training to the Inkatha Freedom Party (IFP), which had been promoting the violent activities of groups of Zulu workers during the transition to democracy. Often, paramilitary groups are associated with particular extremist parties or political factions. In Georgia, after independence, each political party, except the Greens, had its own militia; after his recall to power, Eduard Shevardnadze tried to re-establish a monopoly over the means of violence by welding together these militias into a regular army. It was this ragbag of armed bands that was defeated by a combination of the Abkhazian National Guard and Russian military units in Abkhazia.

The paramilitary groups are mostly composed of redundant soldiers, or even whole units of redundant or breakaway soldiers which sometimes include common criminals, as in the former Yugoslavia where many were deliberately released from prison for the purpose, and unemployed young men in search of a living, a cause or an adventure. They rarely wear uniforms, which makes them difficult to distinguish from non-combatants, although they often wear distinctive clothing or signs. Symbols of global material culture often serve as important quasi-uniforms; for example, Rayban sunglasses, Adidas shoes, jogging suits and caps. The use of child soldiers is not uncommon in Africa; there have also been reports of fourteen-year-old boys operating in Serbian units. In Charles Taylor's National Patriotic Front of Liberia, for example, which invaded Sierra Leone on Christmas Eve 1989, some 30 per cent of the soldiers were said to be under the age of seventeen; Taylor even created a 'Boys' Own Unit'. He supported an invasion of Sierra Leone by a rather small number of rebels, after which the Sierra Leone government recruited large numbers of citizens into its army, including boys some of whom were as young as eight years old: 'Many of the boys recruited into the government army were street-children from Freetown, involved in petty theft before their recruitment. Now they were given an AK47 and a chance to engage in theft on a larger scale.'[3] RENAMO (Resistência Nacional Mocambiçana – the movement founded by Portuguese special forces after the independence of Mozambique and supported by South Africa) also recruited children, some of whom were forced to return to their own villages and attack their families.

Self-defence units are composed of volunteers who try to defend their localities. These would include local brigades in Bosnia–Herzegovina who tried to defend all the citizens of their locality, for example in Tuzla; self-defence units of both Hutus and Tutsis who tried to stop the massacres in 1994; or the self-defence units in South Africa set up by the African National Congress (ANC) to defend localities from Inkatha. Such units are very difficult to sustain mainly because of inadequate resources. Where they are not defeated, they often end up by cooperating with other armed groups and getting sucked into the conflict.

Foreign mercenaries include both individuals on contract to particular fighting units as well as mercenary bands. The former include former Russian officers working on contract with the new post-Soviet armies, and British and French soldiers made redundant by the post-Cold War cuts, who train, advise and even command armed groups in Bosnia, Croatia and various African countries. The most well-known mercenary bands are the *Mujahidiin*, veterans from the Afghan war, generally to be found in all conflicts involving Islam, funded by the Islamic states, most notably Iran. A new phenomenon is private security companies, often recruited from retired soldiers from Britain or the United States, who are hired both by governments and by multinational companies and are often interconnected. Particularly notorious examples are the South African mercenary company Executive Outcomes and the British company Sandline International. Sandline International became famous as a result of the scandal concerning arms sales to Sierra Leone in early 1998. Executive Outcomes has been credited with considerable military success in defending diamond mines in Sierra Leone and Angola. In February 1997 the government of Papua New Guinea hired Sandline International to launch a military assault against the secessionist Bourgainville Revolutionary Army (BRA) and to reopen the Bourgainville copper mine; Sandline International subcontracted the work to Executive Outcomes.[4]

The final category is regular foreign troops operating under the umbrella of international organizations, mainly the UN but also NATO in Bosnia, ECOMOG (Economic Community of West African States Ceasefire Monitoring Group) in Liberia, and the CIS (Commonwealth of Independent States) or OSCE, which have both provided umbrellas for different Russian peacekeeping operations. In general, these troops are not directly involved in the war, although their presence is very significant and I will discuss their role in chapter 6. In some cases, these troops have become involved by fighting, as in the case of ECOMOG in Liberia and Sierra Leone or in the case of Russian peacekeepers in Tadjikistan, and, in such cases, they have taken on some of the characteristics of the other fighting units.

While the small-scale character of the fighting units has much in common with guerrilla warfare, they lack the hierarchy, order and vertical command systems that have been typical of guerrilla forces and that were borrowed from modern warfare as well as the structure of Leninist or Maoist political parties. These various groups operate both independently and in cooperation. What appear to be armies are actually horizontal coalitions of breakaway units from the regular armed forces, local militia or self-defence units, criminal gangs, groups of fanatics, and hangers-on, who have negotiated partnerships, common projects, divisions of labour or spoils. Robert Reich's concept of the 'spider's web' to characterize the new global corporate structure, which I referred to in the previous chapter (see p. 73), is probably also applicable to the new warfare.

Because of cost, logistics and inadequate infrastructure and skills, these 'armies' rarely use heavy weapons, although where they are used they may well make a considerable difference. The Serbian monopoly of heavy artillery was important in Bosnia, as was the intervention of Russian units with aircraft and artillery in Abkhazia. One of the reasons given for the success of Executive Outcomes has been their ability 'to carry out sophisticated operations such as flying helicopter gun ships and light ground-attack fixed-wing aircraft'.[5]

For the most part, light weapons are used – rifles, machine-guns, hand-grenades, landmines and, at the upper end of the scale, low-calibre artillery and short-range rockets. Although these weapons are often described as 'low-tech', they are the product of a long and sophisticated technological evolution. Compared with World War II, they are much lighter, easier to use and transport, more accurate and more difficult to detect. In contrast to heavy weapons, they can be used to great effect by unskilled soldiers, including children. Modern communications are also very important to enable the fighting groups to cooperate, especially radios and mobile telephones. US forces in Somalia were unable to eavesdrop the commercially bought cellular phones used by Somali militiamen.

The end of the Cold War and of related conflicts like Afghanistan or South Africa greatly increased the availability of surplus weapons. In some cases, wars are fought with weapons raided from Cold War stockpiles; such is largely the case in Bosnia–Herzegovina. In other cases, redundant soldiers sell their weapons on the black market, or small-scale producers (as in Pakistan) copy their designs. In addition, arms enterprises which have lost state markets seek new sources of demand. Certain conflicts, for example Kashmir, took on a new character as a result of the influx of arms, in this case a spill over from the conflict in Afghanistan. The new wars could be viewed as a form of military waste-disposal – a way of using up unwanted surplus arms generated by the Cold War, the biggest military build-up in history.

Patterns of Violence

The techniques of the new fighting units owe much to the types of warfare that developed during and after the Second World

War as a reaction to modern war. Revolutionary warfare, as articulated by Mao Tse-tung and Che Guevara, developed tactics that were designed to find a way round large-scale concentrations of conventional forces and that were almost quite counter to conventional strategic theory.

The central objective of revolutionary warfare is the control of territory through gaining support of the local population rather than through capturing territory from enemy forces. The zones under revolutionary control are usually in remote parts of the country which cannot be easily reached by the central administration. They provide bases from which the military forces can engage in tactics which sap the morale and efficiency of enemy forces. Revolutionary warfare has some similarities with manoeuvre theory. It involves decentralized dispersed military activity, with a great emphasis on surprise and mobility. But a key feature of revolutionary warfare is the avoidance of head-on collisions which guerrilla units are likely to lose because of inferior numbers and equipment. Strategic retreats are frequent. According to Mao Tse-tung: 'The ability to run away is precisely one of the characteristics of guerrillas. Running away is the chief means of getting out of passivity and regaining the initiative.'[6]

Great stress is placed by all revolutionary writers on winning 'hearts and minds' not just in the territory under revolutionary control, but in enemy territory as well so that the guerrilla can operate, according to Mao's well-known dictum, 'like a fish in the sea', although, of course, terroristic methods were also used. Counterinsurgency, which has been an almost universal failure,[7] was designed to counter this type of warfare using conventional military forces. The main strategy has been to destroy the environment in which the revolutionaries operate, to poison the sea for the fish. Techniques like forcible resettlement developed by the French in Algeria, or area destruction through scattering mines or herbicides or napalm developed by the Americans in Vietnam, have also been used by, for example, the Indonesians in East Timor or the Turkish government against the Kurds.

The new warfare borrows from both revolutionary warfare and counterinsurgency. It borrows from revolutionary warfare the strategy of controlling territory through political control rather than through capturing territory from enemy forces. This is somewhat easier than it was for revolutionary forces, since in most cases the central authority is very weak and the main contenders for the control of territory are not governments with conventional modern forces but rather similar types of fighting units, even if they bear the name of regular armies. Nevertheless, as in the case of revolutionary warfare, the various factions continue to avoid battle mainly in order to conserve men and equipment. Strategic retreats are typical and ground is conceded to what appears to be the stronger party. Often, the various factions cooperate in dividing up territory between them.

An important difference between revolutionaries and the new warriors, however, is the method of political control. For the revolutionaries, ideology was very important; even though fear was a significant element, popular support and allegiance to the revolutionary idea was the central aim. Hence, the revolutionaries tried to build model societies in the areas under their control. In contrast, the new warriors establish political control through allegiance to a label rather than an idea. In the brave new democratized world, where political mobilization is based on labels and where elections and referenda are often forms of census-taking, this means that the majority of people living in the territory under control must admit to the right label. Anyone else has to be eliminated. Indeed, even in nondemocratized areas, fear of opposition, dissidence or insurgency reinforces this demand for homogeneity of population based on identity.

This is why the main method of territorial control is not popular support, as in the case of revolutionary warfare, but population displacement – getting rid of all possible opponents. To achieve this, the new warfare borrows from counterinsurgency techniques for poisoning the sea – techniques which were refined by guerrilla movements created or promoted by Western governments with experience of counterinsurgency to topple left-wing governments in the 'low-intensity' conflicts of the 1980s such as RENAMO in Mozambique, the *Mujahidiin* in Afghanistan, or the Contras in Nicaragua. Indeed, this approach was a reaction to the failure of counterinsurgency in Vietnam and Southern Africa and the implicit realization that a conventional modern war is no longer a viable option.

Instead of creating a favourable environment for the guerrilla, the new warfare aims to create an unfavourable environment for all those people it cannot control. Control of one's own side depends not on positive benefits, since in the impoverished, disorderly conditions of the new warfare, there is not much that can be offered. Rather, it depends on continuing fear and insecurity and on the perpetuation of hatred of the other. Hence the importance of extreme and conspicuous atrocity and of involving as many people as possible in these crimes so as to establish a shared complicity, to sanction violence against a hated 'other' and to deepen divisions.

The techniques of population displacement include:

1   Systematic murder of those with different labels, as in Rwanda. The killing of Tutsis in 1994 was directed by government officials and the army. According to Human Rights Watch: 'In such places as the commune of Nyakizu in Southern Rwanda, local officials and other killers came to "work" every morning. After they had put in a full day's "work" killing Tutsi, they went home "singing" at quitting time . . . The "workers" returned each day until the job had been finished – that is, until all the Tutsi had been killed.'[8]

2   Ethnic cleansing, that is to say, forcible population expulsion, as in Bosnia–Herzegovina (see chapter 3) or the Transcaucasus. In Abkhazia, another example, the Abkhaz inhabitants accounted for only 17 per cent of the population. In order to control the territory, the secessionist forces had to expel most of the remaining population, mainly Georgian.

3   Rendering an area uninhabitable. This can be done physically, through scattering anti-personnel landmines or through the use of shells and rockets against civilian targets, especially homes, hospitals or crowded places like markets or water sources. It can be done economically through forced famines or sieges. By depriving the people of their livelihood, they either die of hunger as in Southern Sudan, or they are forced to migrate. And it can be done psychologically by instilling unbearable memories of what was once home, by desecrating whatever has social meaning. One method is the destruction of history and culture by removing the physical landmarks that define the social environment for particular groups of people. The destruction of religious buildings and historic monuments is supposed to erase all traces of cultural claim to a particular area. In Banja Luka, at the height of the war, the Serbs

destroyed all seventeen mosques and all but one of the Catholic churches. In particular, they demolished two very beautiful sixteenth-century mosques; they were demolished on a Friday, and on Monday the ground was razed and turfed over. Another method is defilement through systematic rape and sexual abuse which is characteristic of several wars, or by other public and very visible acts of brutality. Psychological methods have the advantage of differentiating between people with different labels.

All of these techniques fall within the definition of genocide contained in the 1948 Geneva Convention. Article 2 reads:

> In the present Convention, genocide means any of the following acts committed with intent to destroy, in whole or in part, a national, racial, or religious group as such: a) Killing members of the group; b) Causing serious bodily or mental harm to members of the group; c) Deliberately inflicting on the group conditions of life calculated to bring about its physical destruction in whole or in part; d) Imposing measures intended to prevent births within the group; e) Forcibly transferring the children of the group to another group.[9]

Essentially, what were considered to be undesirable and illegitimate side-effects of old war have become central to the mode of fighting in the new wars. It is sometimes said that the new wars are a reversion to primitivism. But primitive wars were highly ritualistic and hedged in by social constraints. These wars are rational in the sense that they apply rational thinking to the aims of war and refuse normative constraints.

The pattern of violence in the new type of warfare is confirmed by the statistics of the new wars. The tendency to avoid battle and to direct most violence against civilians is evidenced by the dramatic increase in the ratio of civilian to military casualties. At the beginning of the twentieth century, 85–90 per cent of casualties in war were military. In World War II, approximately half of all war deaths were civilian. By the late 1990s, the proportions of a hundred years ago have been almost exactly reversed, so that nowadays approximately 80 per cent of all casualties in wars are civilian.[10]

The importance of population displacement is evidenced by the figures on refugees and displaced persons. According to

UNHCR, the global refugee population has risen from 2.4 million people in 1975 to 10.5 million people in 1985 and 14.4 million people in 1995 (a decline from 18.2 million in 1992 due to the repatriation of some 9 million people). This figure only includes refugees who cross international boundaries. According to the same figures, another 5.4 million people are internally displaced.[11] Figures provided by the US Committee on Refugees are much higher, increasing from 22 million in 1980 to 38 million in 1995, of whom approximately half were internally displaced persons.[12] Using the latter figures, Myron Weiner has calculated that the number of refugees per conflict has roughly doubled since 1969, increasing from 287,000 per conflict to 459,000 per conflict in 1992. But the increase in internally displaced persons has shown an even more dramatic increase, from 40,000 per conflict in 1969 to 857,000 per conflict in 1992.[13]

Financing the War Effort

The new wars take place in a context which could be represented as an extreme version of globalization. Territorially-based production more or less collapses either as a result of liberalization and the withdrawal of state support, or through physical destruction (pillage, shelling, etc.), or because markets are cut off as a result of the disintegration of states, fighting, or deliberate blockades imposed by outside powers, or more likely, by fighting units on the ground, or because spare parts, raw material and fuel are impossible to acquire. In some cases, a few valuable commodities continue to be produced – e.g. diamonds in Angola and Sierra Leone, lapis lazuli and emeralds in Afghanistan, drugs in Colombia and Tadjikistan – and they provide a source of income for whoever can provide 'protection'. Unemployment is very high and, as long as governments continue to spend, inflation is rampant. In extreme cases, the currency collapses to be replaced by barter, the use of valuable commodities as currency or the circulation of foreign currencies, dollars or deutschmarks.

Given the erosion of the tax base both because of the collapse of production and because of the difficulties of collection, governments, like privatized military groups, need to seek alternative sources of funding in order to sustain their violent activities. Given the collapse of productive activity, the main sources of funding are either what Mark Duffield calls 'asset transfer',[14] i.e. the redistribution of existing assets so as to favour the fighting units, or external assistance. The simplest form of asset transfer is loot, robbery, extortion, pillage and hostage-taking. This is widespread in all contemporary wars. Rich people are killed and their gold and valuables stolen; property is transferred in the aftermath of ethnic cleansing; cattle and livestock are raided by militiamen;[15] shops and factories are looted when towns are taken. Hostages are captured and exchanged for food, weapons or other hostages, prisoners of war or dead bodies.

A second form of asset transfer is market pressure. A typical characteristic of the new wars are the numerous checkpoints which control the supply of food and necessities. Sieges and blockades, the division of territory between different paramilitary groups, allow the fighting units to control market prices. Thus a typical pattern, observed in Sudan, former Yugoslavia and other places, is that urban dwellers or even farmers will be forced to sell their assets – cars, fridges, televisions or cows – at ridiculously low prices in exchange for highly priced necessities simply in order to survive.

More sophisticated income-generating activities include 'war taxes' or 'protection' money from the production of primary commodities and various forms of illegal trading. The production and sale of drugs is a key source of income in Colombia, Peru and Tadjikistan. It is estimated that income from drugs accounts for 70 per cent of the opposition revenue in Tadjikistan, while the income of the Colombian guerrillas is said to amount to some $US800 million a year, which compares with government defence expenditure of $US1.4 billion.[16] Trading in drugs, arms or laundered money, and sanctions busting are all examples of revenue-raising criminal activities in which the various military groups are engaged.

However, given the collapse of domestic production, external assistance is crucial, since arms, ammunition, food, not to mention Mercedes cars or Rayban sunglasses, have to be imported. External assistance can take the following forms:

1   Remittances from abroad to individual families, for exam-

ple, Sudanese or Palestinian workers in the oil-rich countries of the Middle East, Bosnian and Croatian workers in
Germany or Austria. These remittances can be converted
into military resources through the various forms of asset
transfer described above.

2   Direct assistance from the diaspora living abroad. This includes material assistance, arms and money, for example
from Irish Americans to the IRA, from Armenians all over
the world to Nagorno-Karabakh, from Canadian Croatians
to the ruling Croatian party and so on.

3   Assistance from foreign governments. During the Cold War
period, both regular forces and guerrillas relied on their superpower patrons. This source of assistance has largely dried
up although the USA still provides support to a number of
governments. Neighbouring states often provide support to
particular factions, to support minorities or because of the
presence of large numbers of refugees or because of involvement in various types of (illegal) trading arrangements. Thus
Serbia and Croatia have provided support to their client
statelets in Bosnia Herzegovina; Armenia supported
Nagorno-Karabakh; Russia has supported a variety of secessionist movements on its borders, whether as a way of
re-establishing control over post-Soviet space, or because
of mafia or military vested interests is a matter for speculation; Rwanda supported the opposition in Zaire as a way of
preventing Hutu militiamen from operating from refugee
camps there; and Uganda supported the Rwandan Patriotic
Front which took over after the massacres of 1994 and continues to support the SPLA in Southern Sudan (and, in return, the Sudanese government supports the Lord's
Resistance Army in Uganda). Other foreign governments
that provide support include former colonial powers concerned about 'stability', for example France and Belgium in
Central Africa, or Islamic states.

4   Humanitarian assistance. There are various ways in which
both governments and warring factions divert humanitarian assistance for their own use. Indeed, donors regard a
5 per cent diversion of humanitarian aid as acceptable in
view of the needs of the most vulnerable parts of the population. The most common method is 'customs duties'. The
Bosnian Croats demanded 27 per cent for humanitarian

assistance transported through so-called Herzeg–Bosne, which, at the height of the war, was the only way to reach certain areas in Central Bosnia. But there are also other ways, including robbery and ambush. By insisting on the use of an overvalued official exchange rate, both the Sudanese and Ethiopian governments were able to profit from the provision of humanitarian aid.

Essentially, the fragmentation and informalization of war is paralleled by the informalization of the economy. In place of the national formal economy with its emphasis on industrial production and state regulation, a new type of globalized informal economy is established in which external flows, especially humanitarian assistance and remittances from abroad are integrated into a local and regional economy based on asset transfer and extra-legal trading. Figure 5.1 illustrates the typical resource flows of a new war. It is assumed that there is no production and no taxation. Instead, external support to ordinary people, in the form of remittances and humanitarian assistance, is recycled via various forms of asset transfer and black-market trading into military resources. Direct assistance from foreign governments, protection money from producers of commodities and assistance from the diaspora enhance the capacity of the various fighting units to extract further resources from ordinary people and thus sustain their military efforts.

Mark Duffield describes how this functioned in the Sudanese case where an illegal dollar trade involving Sudan, Zaire and Uganda was operated, making use of relief convoys both for transport and to control prices:

In the case of Sudan, the parallel economy consists of a number of interconnecting levels or systems. Local asset transfer is linked to national level extra-legal mercantile activity. In turn, this articulates with higher-level political and state relations together with regional and international parallel networks which trade in commodities and hard currency. It is this level that provides the initial site for the integration of international aid and relief assistance with the parallel economy. As assets flow upwards and outwards, culminating in capital flight, international assistance flows downwards through the same or related systems of power.[17]

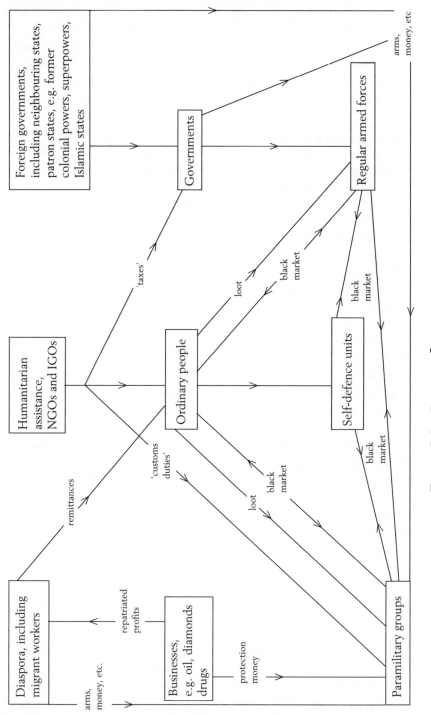

Figure 5.1 *Resource flows in new wars*

Foreign governments, including neighbouring states, patron states, e.g. former colonial powers, superpowers, Islamic states

Governments

Regular armed forces

arms, money, etc

'taxes'

Humanitarian assistance, NGOs and IGOs

Ordinary people

loot

black market

Self-defence units

black market

black market

'customs duties'

remittances

Diaspora, including migrant workers

arms, money, etc.

repatriated profits

Businesses, e.g. oil, diamonds drugs

protection money

loot

black market

black market

Paramilitary groups

Just as it is possible to find examples of military cooperation between fighting units so as to divide up territory or to foster mutual hatred among the respective populations, so it is possible to find examples of economic cooperation. David Keen describes what is known as the 'sell-game' in Sierra Leone, through which government forces sell arms and ammunition to the rebels:

> [Government forces] withdraw from a town, leaving arms and ammunition for the rebels behind them. The rebels pick up the arms and extract the loot, mostly in the form of cash, from the townspeople and then they themselves retreat. At this point, the government forces reoccupy the town and engage in their own looting, usually of property (which the rebels find hard to dispose of) as well as engaging in illegal mining.[18]

John Simpson describes how Peruvian government soldiers set free captured Shining Path guerrillas 'apparently in order to perpetuate insecurity in areas where officers can benefit from illegal trading – in this case, principally the trade in cocaine.'[19] There are similar examples in the Bosnian war which I have described in chapter 3.

Some writers argue that economic motivation explains the new type of warfare. David Keen suggests that a 'war where one avoids battles but picks on unarmed civilians and perhaps eventually acquires a Mercedes may make more sense . . . [than] risking death in the name of the nation-state with little or no prospect of significant financial gain'.[20] But economic motivation alone is insufficient to explain the scale, brutality and sheer viciousness of new wars.[21] No doubt some join the fighting as a way of legitimizing criminal activities, providing a political justification for what they do and socially sanctioning otherwise illegal methods of financial gain. No doubt there are others – rational power-seekers, extreme fanatics or victims intent on revenge – who engage in criminal activities to sustain their political military goals. Yet others are press-ganged into the fighting, propelled by fear and hunger.

The point is rather that the modern distinctions between the political and the economic, the public and the private, the military and the civil are breaking down. Political control is required to embed the new coercive forms of economic exchange, which in turn are required to provide a viable financial basis for the new gangsters/powerholders in the context of state disintegration and economic marginalization. A new retrograde set of social relationships is being established in which economics and violence are deeply intertwined within the shared framework of identity politics.

The Spread of Violence

The new type of warfare is a predatory social condition.[22] While it may be possible to contain particular groups or individuals, it is very difficult to contain the social condition either in space or in time. Neighbouring countries are the most immediately affected. The cost of the war in terms of lost trade, especially where sanctions or communications blockades are introduced or where borders are closed, either deliberately or because of fighting; the burden of refugees, since generally it is the neighbouring states who accept the largest numbers; the spread of illegal circuits of trade; and the spill-over of identity politics – all these factors reproduce the conditions that nurture the new forms of violence.

The NGO Saferworld has enumerated the cost of conflict to neighbouring countries in several cases. One example is the war in Mozambique, which was an important trade route for landlocked countries like Zambia, Zimbabwe, Malawi, Botswana and Swaziland. Malawi lost all its trade with Mozambique, and the additional costs of transport during the height of the war were estimated at 11 per cent of annual export earnings; likewise, trade with Zimbabwe fell dramatically and the cost of rerouting goods through South Africa was estimated at $US825 million in 1988 prices.[23] In the Balkans, the decline in GDP following the wars in Croatia and Bosnia–Herzegovina, as a result of the loss of trade due to the closure of borders and to sanctions and the increased cost of transportation, was more or less inversely proportionate to distance from the epicentre of violence. The decline in GDP in Bosnia–Herzegovina was most dramatic, falling from $US2,719 per head before the war broke out to just $US250 per head when the war ended. Surrounding Bosnia–Herzegovina is an inner ring of countries – Serbia/Montenegro, Croatia, and Macedonia – whose GDPs fell to 49 per cent, 65 per cent and 55 per cent of their 1989 levels, respectively. By 1996, Serbia/Montenegro and Macedonia had just managed to arrest the decline, while Croatia was able to achieve a very small growth rate. Surrounding these three countries is an outer ring of further affected countries – Albania, Bulgaria, Romania and Slovenia – whose GDPs fell to 81 per cent, 88 per cent, 73 per cent and 90 per cent of their 1989 levels. Finally, the outermost ring – Hungary, Greece and Turkey – all also reported economic losses due to the war.[24]

As well as direct economic costs, it is the neighbouring countries that bear the main burden of refugees. Most refugees are based in neighbouring countries. According to UNHCR figures, out of the 14.5 million refugees recorded for 1995, the majority (6.7 million and 5.0 million respectively) are based in Africa and Asia. Countries hosting more than 500,000 refugees include Guinea (from Liberia and Sierra Leone), Sudan (mainly from Ethiopia, Eritrea and Chad), Tanzania (mainly from Rwanda and Burundi), Zaire (which had, as of 1995, received 1.7 million refugees of whom 1.2 million came from Rwanda and the remainder mainly from Angola, Burundi and Sudan), Iran (from Afghanistan and Iraq), Pakistan (also from Afghanistan and Iraq), Germany (mainly from the former Yugoslavia) and the United States. In Europe, after Germany, the biggest recipients of refugees have been Croatia and Serbia/Montenegro. Not only are these huge concentrations of refugees an immense economic burden on countries that are already poor, but they represent a permanent source of tension between the refugees and the host populations – for economic reasons, since they are competing for resources; for political reasons, since they constitute a permanent pressure on host governments to take action in order that they can return; and for security reasons, because the camps are often used as bases for various radical factions. The most long-standing example of both economic and political burdens are the Palestinian refugees squashed into the West Bank and Gaza or based in Jordan and the Lebanon. As in the case of the Palestinian refugees, up to a million or so Azeri refugees from Nagorno-Karabakh in Azerbaijan, or the Georgian IDPs (internally displaced persons) from Abkhazia in Georgia or the refugee and IDPs in the former Yugoslav republics all constitute a permanent source of political pressure for radical action. In Zaire, the Hutu refugee camps served as a base for Hutu militiamen and contributed to the mobilization of Zairian Tutsis against the Mobutu regime.

Illegal circuits of trade are another conduit for the spread of the new type of war economy. Trade routes necessarily cross borders. The instability in Albania in the mid-1990s was mainly the consequence of the growth of mafia groups well connected to the ruling circles involved in sanctions-busting to Serbia/Montenegro and gun-running to Bosnia–Herzegovina. The pyramid schemes that collapsed so dramatically were used to finance these activities – a classic case of asset transfer. The huge transfer of arms by the United States to Afghan guerrilla groups in the 1980s (much of which was largely diverted) transformed itself into networks of arms and drug trade covering Afghanistan, Pakistan, Kashmir and Tadjikistan.[25] Mark Duffield shows how the illegal dollar trade linked to the war in Sudan involved 'Zairois with gold wanting imported goods, food and fuel; Sudanese with dollars wanting food, clothing and coffee; and Ugandans with imported goods wanting gold and dollars for Kampala's parallel markets.'[26]

Finally, the politics of identity, itself, has a tendency to spread. All identity-based groups, whether defined in terms of language, religion or some other form of differentiation, spill over borders; after all, it is precisely the heterogeneity of identities that offers the opportunity for various forms of exclusivism. Majorities in one country are minorities in another: Tutsis in Rwanda, Burundi and Zaire; Russians in most post-Soviet states, especially so-called Cossacks on the borders of Russia; Islamic groups in central Asia – these are among the many vectors through which identity politics passes.

It is possible to identify spreading regional clusters characterized by this predatory social condition of the new war economies. Myron Weiner calls them 'Bad Neighbourhoods'. The clearest examples are the Balkan region surrounding Bosnia–Herzegovina; the Caucasus stretching south from Chechnya as far as Western Turkey and Northern Iran; the Horn of Africa, including Ethiopia, Eritrea, Somalia and Sudan; Central Africa, especially Rwanda, Burundi and Zaire; the West African countries surrounding Liberia and Sierra Leone; and Central Asia, from Tadjikistan to India. The countries hosting Palestinian refugees might be treated as another cluster; since Israel made peace with the neighbouring states, the conflict is no longer expressed in terms of interstate war and has begun to exhibit some of the characteristics of the new types of conflict.

Conclusion

The new wars have political goals. The aim is political mobilization on the basis of identity. The military strategy for achieving
this aim is population displacement and destabilization so as to
get rid of those whose identity is different and to foment hatred
and fear. Nevertheless, this divisive and exclusive form of politics cannot be disentangled from its economic basis. The various
political/military factions plunder the assets of ordinary people
as well as the remnants of the state and cream off external assistance destined for the victims, in a way that is only possible in
conditions of war or near war. In other words, war provides a
legitimation for various criminal forms of private aggrandize-
ment while at the same time these are necessary sources of revenue in order to sustain the war. The warring parties need more
or less permanent conflict both to reproduce their positions of
power and for access to resources.

While this predatory set of social relationships is most preva-
lent in the war zones, it also characterizes the surrounding regions. Because participation in the war is relatively low (in Bosnia,
only 6.5 per cent of the population took part directly in the prosecution of the war) the difference between zones of war and apparent zones of peace are not nearly as marked as in earlier periods.
Just as it is difficult to distinguish between the political and the
economic, public and private, military and civil, so it is increasingly difficult to distinguish between war and peace. The new war
economy could be represented as a continuum, starting with the
combination of criminality and racism to be found in the inner
cities of Europe and North America and reaching its most acute
manifestation in the areas where the scale of violence is greatest.

If violence and predation are to be found in what are considered zones of peace, so it is possible to find islands of civility in
nearly all the war zones. They are much less known about than
the war zones, because it is violence and criminality and not
normality that is generally reported. But there are regions where
local state apparatuses continue to function, where taxes are
raised, services are provided and some production is maintained.
There are groups who defend humanistic values and refuse the
politics of particularism. The town of Tuzla in Bosnia–
Herzegovina represents one celebrated example. The self-

defence units created in Southern Rwanda are another example. In isolation, these islands of civility are difficult to preserve, squeezed by the polarization of violence, but the very fragmentary and decentralized character of the new type of warfare makes such examples possible.

Precisely because the new wars are a social condition that arises as the formal political economy withers, they are very difficult to end. Diplomatic negotiations from above fail to take into account the underlying social relations; they treat the various factions as though they were proto-states. Temporary ceasefires or truces may merely legitimize new agreements or partnerships that, for the moment, suit the various factions. Peacekeeping troops sent in to monitor ceasefires which reflect the status quo may help to maintain a division of territory and to prevent the return of refugees. Economic reconstruction channelled through existing 'political authorities' may merely provide new sources of revenue as local assets dry up. As long as the power relations remain the same, sooner or later the violence will start again.

Fear, hatred and predation are not recipes for long-term viable polities. Indeed, this type of war economy is perennially on the edge of exhaustion. This does not mean, however, that they will disappear of their own accord. There has to be some alternative. In the next chapter, I will consider the possibilities for such an alternative; in particular, how islands of civility might offer a counterlogic to the new warfare.

6

Towards a Cosmopolitan Approach

At the beginning of the 1990s, there was a lot of optimism about the possibilities for solving global problems, particularly wars. In the *Agenda for Peace*, the UN Secretary General Boutros Boutros-Ghali talked about the 'second chance' for the UN now its activities were no longer blocked by the Cold War. The term 'international community', implying a cohesive group of governments acting through international organizations, entered into everyday usage. A number of conflicts seemed close to resolution – Cambodia, Namibia, Angola, South Africa, Nicaragua, Afghanistan. And in those conflicts which were not resolved, the idea, enunciated by the French Minister and former director of Médecins Sans Frontières Bernard Kouchner, of a right–duty to intervene for humanitarian purposes seemed to be gaining widespread acceptance.

The number of UN peacekeeping operations increased dramatically in the 1990s, as did the range of tasks they were asked to perform, including the delivery of humanitarian aid, the protection of people in safe havens, disarmament and demobilization, creating a secure environment for elections, reporting violations of international humanitarian law, in addition to the traditional tasks of monitoring and maintaining ceasefires. Mandates were also strengthened; in both Somalia and Bosnia, peacekeeping troops were authorized to act under Chapter VII of the UN Charter which allows the use of force. Moreover, the UN was not the only umbrella for multilateral peacekeeping operations; regional organizations like NATO, the CIS or the Economic Community of West African States (ECOWAS) were also responsible for organizing peacekeeping missions.

Yet despite the hopes and good intentions, the experience so far of what has come to be known as humanitarian intervention has been frustrating, to say the least. At best, people have been fed and fragile ceasefires have been agreed, although it is not clear whether this can be attributed to the presence of peace-keeping troops. At worst, the UN has been shamed and humili-ated, as, for example, when it failed to prevent genocide in Rwanda, when the so-called safe haven of Srebrenica was over-run by Bosnian Serbs, or when the hunt for the Somali warlord Aideed ended in a mixture of farce and tragedy.

There have been many explanations for the failures – the short-termism of politicians, the role of the media which raises public consciousness at particular times and particular places, the lack of coordination of governments and international agencies, in-adequate resources – and all of these have some merit. But the most important explanation is misperception, the persistence of inherited ways of thinking about organized violence, the inabil-ity to understand the character and logic of the new warfare. One response to the new wars has been to treat them as Clausewitzean wars in which the warring parties are states, or if not states, groups with a claim to statehood. Many of the terms used, like 'intervention', 'peacekeeping', 'peace-enforcement', 'sovereignty', 'civil war', are drawn from conceptions of the na-tion-state and of modern war that are not only difficult to apply in the current context, but may actually pose an obstacle to ap-propriate action. The other response is fatalistic. Because the wars cannot be understood in traditional terms, they are thought to represent a reversion to primitivism or anarchy and the most that can be done, therefore, is to ameliorate the symptoms. In other words, wars are treated as natural disasters; hence the use of terms like 'complex emergencies', which are emptied of po-litical meaning. Indeed the very term 'humanitarian' has acquired a non-political meaning in the 1990s. It has come to be associ-ated with the provision of humanitarian relief assistance in wars, or help to non-combatants or the wounded, rather than with respect for human rights which was implied in the classic usage of the term 'humanitarian intervention'.[1]

The analysis in the previous chapters implies a different

approach towards trying to solve these conflicts. What is needed is much more political response to the new wars. A strategy of capturing 'hearts and minds' needs to be counterposed to the strategy of sowing 'fear and hate'. A politics of inclusion needs to be counterposed against the politics of exclusion; respect for international principles and legal norms needs to be counterposed against the criminality of the warlords. In short, what is needed is a new form of cosmopolitan political mobilization, which embraces both the so-called international community and local populations, and which is capable of countering the submission to various types of particularism. A sceptic might argue that a form of cosmopolitan politics is already on the international agenda; certainly, respect for human rights, abhorrence of genocide and ethnic cleansing are increasingly part of the accepted rhetoric of political leaders. But political mobilization involves more than this; it has to override other considerations – geopolitics or short-term domestic concerns; it has to constitute the primary guide to policy and action which has not been the case up to now.

In this chapter, I develop this argument, first with some general considerations about the construction of legitimacy and the terminology of humanitarian intervention and, second, I will explore what a cosmopolitan approach might mean in political, military and economic terms.

The Reconstruction of Legitimacy

The key to the control of violence is the reconstruction of legitimacy. I agree with Hannah Arendt when she says that power rests on legitimacy and not on violence. By legitimacy, I mean both consent and even support for political institutions, as well as the notion that these institutions acquire their authority on the basis of operating within an agreed set of rules – the rule of law. Arendt claims that:

> No government exclusively based on the means of violence has ever existed . . . Single men without others to support them never have enough power to use violence successfully. Hence, in domestic affairs, violence functions as the last resort of power against criminals or rebels – that is, against single individuals who, as it

were, refuse to be overpowered by the consensus of the majority. And as for actual warfare . . . an enormous superiority in the
means of violence can become helpless if confronted with an ill-
equipped but well-organized opponent who is much more powerful.[2]

The same point is made by Giddens. The internal pacification of
modern states was achieved not by violence, but by the extension of the rule of law and, concomitantly, the administrative
reach of the state, including the extension of surveillance. The
monopoly of legitimate organized violence implied the control
of violence and much less reliance on the use of physical coercion, except, of course, in the international arena. Pre-modern
states were much more violent in domestic affairs than the modern state, but also much less powerful. In so far as external violence contributed to internal pacification, it was an indirect
contribution, arising from the increased legitimacy of the state
associated with the defence of territory from external enemies
and the augmentation of administrative capacities.

In the new wars, the monopoly of legitimate violence has
broken down. And what is crucial is not the privatization of
violence, as such, but the breakdown of legitimacy. As I have
argued in the previous chapter, the goals of the new warfare are
particularistic. The strategy is political control on the basis of
exclusion – in particular, population displacement – and the tactics for achieving this goal are terror and destabilization. For this
reason, it is virtually impossible for any of the warring parties to
re-establish legitimacy. Violence may be controlled sporadically
through uneasy truces and ceasefires, but in situations in which
the moral, administrative and practical constraints against private violence have broken down, they rarely last long. At the
same time, however, isolated citizens' groups or political parties
which try to re-establish legitimacy on the basis of inclusive politics are relatively powerless in conditions of continuing violence.

'Cosmopolitanism', used in a Kantian sense, implies the existence of a human community with certain shared rights and ob-
ligations. In 'Perpetual Peace' Kant envisaged a world federation
of democratic states in which cosmopolitan right is confined to
the right of 'hospitality' – strangers and foreigners should be
welcomed and treated with respect.[3] I use the term more extensively to refer both to a positive political vision, embracing

tolerance, multiculturalism, civility and democracy, and to a more legalistic respect for certain overriding universal principles which should guide political communities at various levels, including the global level.

These principles are already contained in various treaties and conventions that comprise the body of international law. In chapter 2, I referred to the various rules of engagement and laws of war which deal with the abuses of armed power. Laws and customs of war which date back to early modern times were codified in the nineteenth and twentieth centuries; particularly important were the Geneva Conventions sponsored by the ICRC and the Hague Conferences of 1899 and 1907. The Nuremberg trials after the Second World War marked the first enforcement of 'war crimes', or, even more significantly, 'crimes against humanity'. To what was known as international humanitarian law, human rights norms were added in the post-war period. The difference between humanitarian and human rights law has to do largely with whether violation of the law takes place in war or peacetime. The former is confined to abuses of power in wartime situations. The assumption tends to be that war is usually modern interstate war and that such abuses are inflicted by a foreign power – in other words, aggression. The latter is equally concerned with abuses of power in peacetime, in particular those inflicted by a government against its citizens – in other words, repression.[4]

The violations of international norms with which both bodies of law are concerned are, in fact, those which form the core of the new mode of warfare. As I have argued, in the new wars the classic distinctions between internal and external, war and peace, aggression and repression are breaking down. A war crime is at one and the same time a massive violation of human rights. A number of writers have suggested that humanitarian law should be combined with human rights law to form 'humane' or 'cosmopolitan' law.[5] Elements of a cosmopolitan regime do already exist. NGOs and the media draw attention to violations of human rights or to war crimes, and to some extent governments and international institutions respond through methods ranging from persuasion and pressure to, as yet, tentative, enforcement. Particularly important in the latter respect has been the establishment of international tribunals with respect to violations of international humanitarian law for Rwanda and former Yugoslavia, and the creation of an International Criminal Court (ICC) to deal with 'core crimes' – war crimes, crimes against humanity and genocide. War crimes tribunals were established in 1993 and 1994, and the ICC in 1998.

These tentative steps towards a cosmopolitan regime, however, conflict with many of the more traditional geo-political approaches adopted by the so-called international community which continue to emphasize the importance of state sovereignty as the basis of international relations. The prevalence of geo-politics is reflected in the terminology used to describe the response of the international community to post-Cold War conflicts. The literature is replete with discussions about intervention and non-intervention.[6] Intervention is taken to mean an infringement of sovereignty and, in its strong version, a military infringement. The prohibitions against intervention, expressed in particular in Article 2(1) of the UN Charter which refers to the 'principle of sovereign equality', is considered important as a way of restricting the use of force, respecting pluralism and acting 'as a brake on the crusading, territorial and imperial ambitions of states'.[7]

But what does intervention and non-intervention mean nowadays? The new types of war are both global and local. There is already extensive international involvement, both private through diaspora connections, NGOs, etc., and public through patron states or international agencies providing aid or loans or other kinds of assistance. Indeed, as I argued in the previous chapter, the various parties to the conflict are totally dependent on outside support. Likewise, these are wars usually characterized by the erosion or disintegration of state power. In such a situation, what does it mean to talk about infringements of sovereignty?

An illustration of the artificiality of these terms was the debate about whether the war in Bosnia was an international or civil war. Those who argued that this was an international war favoured intervention to support the Bosnian state. They argued that the Bosnian state had been internationally recognized and that the war was the result of an act of aggression by Serbia. Hence, intervention was justified under Chapter VII of the UN Charter since Serbian aggression was a 'threat to international peace and security'. Those who argued that this was a civil war were against intervention. They claimed that this was a nationalist war between Serbs, Croats and Bosnians to control the remnants of the Yugoslav state – intervention would have a been a violation of sovereignty. Both positions missed the point. This was a war of ethnic cleansing and genocide. What did it matter whether the crime was committed by Serbs from Belgrade or by Serbs from Bosnia? What did it matter, in practical terms, whether Yugoslavia was the internationally recognized state or Bosnia? Something had to be done to protect the victims and to uphold respect for international humanitarian norms. In effect, the debate about whether the conflict was an international or civil war treated it as an old war between the fighting sides, in which violence against civilians is merely a side-effect of the war.

Moreover, because outside involvement in various forms is already so extensive in this type of conflict, there is no such thing as non-intervention. The failure to protect the victims is a kind of tacit intervention on the side of those who are inflicting humanitarian or human rights abuses.

It is sometimes argued that intervention only refers to military intervention. Military means are often contrasted with political means as a way of solving conflicts. Behind this distinction is an assumption that these wars are comparable to modern wars. Military intervention implies military support for one side in the conflict. A political approach, on the other hand, implies negotiation between the sides. Hence, the debate about whether the war in Bosnia was an international or civil war was sometimes presented as a debate about military versus political means. Again, this debate missed the point. The question was not whether to use military or political means, but what kind of politics would guide the use of military force. Both the argument for intervention on the side of the Bosnian state and the argument for negotiation which might lead to the use of troops in a peacekeeping role presuppose a traditional geo-political view of the conflict in which the sides to the conflict were proto-states and in which a political solution would emerge either as a result of victory of one side or as a result of a compromise. The solution had to do with the division of territory.

An alternative cosmopolitan approach starts from the assumption that no solution is workable based on the political goals of the warring parties and that legitimacy can only be restored on the basis of an alternative politics which operates within cosmopolitan principles. Once the values of inclusion, tolerance and mutual respect are established, the territorial solutions will easily follow. What this means in practical terms is the subject of the rest of this chapter.

From Top-down Diplomacy to Cosmopolitan Politics

In recent wars, the dominant approach of the international community has been to attempt a negotiated solution between the warring parties. This approach has several drawbacks.

First, the talks raise the profile of the warring parties and confer a sort of public legitimacy on individuals who may be criminals. Many people remarked on the paradox that international negotiators were seen on television shaking hands with Karadžić and Mladić, both of whom had earlier been named by the International Tribunal and by leading Western politicians as war criminals. The same contradiction applied to the involvement of the Khmer Rouge in the Paris talks which led to the agreements to end the war in Cambodia, or the high-profile talks between Mohammed Aideed and Ali Mahdi about the division of Mogadishu shortly after the arrival of US troops in Somalia in December 1992.

Second, because of the particularistic nature of the political goals of the warring parties, it is extremely difficult to find a workable solution. One option is territorial partition – a kind of identity-based apartheid. The other option is power-sharing on the basis of identity. The record of such agreements is dismal. Partitions do not provide a basis for stability; refugees, displaced persons or newly created minorities constitute a long-term source of tension, as the history of partitions in Cyprus, India and Pakistan, Ireland or Palestine testifies.[8] Nor do power-sharing agreements fare any better. The constitutions of both Cyprus and Lebanon offer examples of unworkable compromises which exacerbated ethnic and/or religious competition and mutual suspicion. Today, the Washington Agreement between Croats and Muslims, the Dayton Agreement, the Oslo Agreement between Israel and the Palestinians, or the Paris Agreements on Cambodia are all displaying the strains of trying to combine incompatible forms of exclusivism.

A third drawback is that such agreements tend to be based on exaggerated assumptions about the power of the warring parties to implement agreements. Since the power of the warring parties depends largely on fear and / or self-interest and not on consent, they need an insecure environment to sustain themselves both politically and economically. Politically, identity is based on fear and hatred of the other; economically, revenues depend on outside assistance for the war effort and on various forms of asset transfer based on loot and extortion or on price distortions resulting from restrictions on freedom of movement. In peacetime, these sources of sustenance are eroded.

It is often argued that, despite these drawbacks, there is no alternative. These are the only people who can end the violence. It is true that those responsible for the violence have to end it, but it does not follow that these are the people who can make peace. Negotiations with warlords may sometimes be necessary, but they need to take place in a context where alternative non-exclusive political constituencies can be fostered. The aim is to establish conditions for an alternative political mobilization. This means that the mediators have to be very clear about international principles and standards and refuse compromises that violate those principles, otherwise the credibility of the institutions will suffer and any kind of implementation could be very difficult. The point of the talks is to control violence so that space can be created for the emergence or re-emergence of civil society. The more 'normal' the situation, the greater the possibilities for developing political alternatives. There is, as it were, another potential source of power that has to be represented at the talks, involved or consulted in any compromise and, generally, made more visible. Precisely because these are not total wars, participation is low, loyalties change, sources of revenue dry up, it is always possible to identify local advocates of cosmopolitanism, people and places which refuse to accept the politics of war – islands of civility.

In chapter 3, I described the example of Tuzla in Bosnia–Herzegovina (see p. 55). Northwest Somaliland represents another example where local elders have succeeded in establishing relative peace through a process of negotiation. In Armenia and Azerbaijan, the local branches of the Helsinki Citizens' Assembly have succeeded in negotiating with local authorities on each side of the border, Kazakh and Echevan, and establishing a peace corridor; the corridor provides a place where hostages and prisoners of war can be released and where dialogue between women's groups, young people and even security forces can be organized.

In South Africa, there have been many cases of locally negotiated peace accords during the violence between Inkatha and the ANC. Davin Bremmer has described how the Wilgesprunt Fellowship Centre was able to establish a zone of peace in the Meadowlands Hostel in Soweto, which had been a flashpoint of violence between the IFP and the ANC.[9] In the Mpumalanga community in KwaZulu-Natal, two local leaders representing the two main political factions joined with other residents to form the Peace and Hope Foundation Trust, which provided mediation and other conflict resolution services at a local level, such as a 'rumour control system'.[10] In the Philippines, a peace zones strategy was adopted after a town in the north, Hungduan, convinced guerrillas to withdraw from the town and then acted to prevent the military from moving in; the peace zones strategy is said to have been an important factor in ending the war.[11]

Many other examples from Northern Ireland, Central America, Vojvidina or West Africa can be enumerated. They are rarely reported because they are not news. They involve local negotiations and conflict resolution between local factions, or they may involve pressure on the warring parties to keep out of the area. They are often difficult to sustain because of the pressures of the war economy – influxes of refugees seeking safety, unemployment, propaganda, especially television, radio and video cassettes controlled by the warring parties. But they need to be taken seriously and given credibility by outside support.

These groups represent a potential solution. To the extent that they are capable of mobilizing support, they weaken the power of the warring parties. To the extent that the areas they control can be extended, so the zones of war are diminished. They also represent a repository of knowledge and information about the local situation; they can advise and guide a cosmopolitan strategy.

In many places, there is a growing emphasis by governments and international organizations on the role of local NGOs and grass-roots initiatives, and they provide funding and other forms of support. In some cases, support for NGOs is seen as a substitute for action. They are supposed to undertake the tasks that the international community is unable to fulfil. But what is not understood is that, in a context of war, the survival of such groups is always precarious. Civil society needs a state. If the local state does not provide the conditions in which alternative politics can develop, there has to be support from international organizations. However courageous those engaged in NGOs, they cannot operate without law and order. The peace movement in Bosnia–Herzegovina was destroyed when the Serbs began to shoot demonstrators. What happened in Rwanda is a classic illustration of what happens to local advocates of cosmopolitanism without outside support. According to Alex de Waal:

> Rwanda had an exemplary 'human rights community'. Seven indigenous human rights NGOs collaborated closely with their foreign friends and patrons, providing unrivaled documentation of the ongoing massacres and assassinations . . . They predicted massive atrocities unless named perpetrators were called to account. But there was no 'primary movement' that could underpin the activists' agenda, no political establishment ready to listen to their critique and act on it, and no international organizations ready to take measures and risks necessary to protect them . . . On April 6 1994, the Hutu extremists called the bluff of the human rights community and launched their final solution. As well as eradicating all Tutsis, they embarked upon the systematic assassination of all critics. The UN ran away, while the US government thought up nice excuses for inaction.[12]

Just as the warring factions depend on outside support, so there needs to be a conscious strategy of building on local cosmopolitan initiatives. What form support takes, whether or not it involves sending troops, depends on each situation and what the local groups consider necessary. But there is still a reluctance to engage in a serious dialogue on a par with the dialogue with the warring parties, to see these groups as partners in a shared cosmopolitan project and to work out jointly a mutual strategy for developing a peace constituency. There is a tendency on the part of Western political leaders to dismiss such initiatives as worthy but insignificant; 'citizens can't make peace', said David Owen when negotiator in the former Yugoslavia. This attitude can perhaps be explained by the horizontal character of top-level communication, the fact that leaders generally only talk to leaders. It also has to do with the colonial mentality that seems to grip representatives of international institutions when on missions in faraway countries – there are widespread complaints, whether in Somalia, Bosnia or the Transcaucasus, about the seemingly systematic failure to consult local experts or NGOs.

A Somali driver in Mogadishu commented on the negotiations between Mohammed Aideed and Ali Mahdi in the following terms:

> Everyone agrees that these men have caused so much unnecessary suffering in this country. We understand that the US Embassy had to deal with these men. But did the embrace have to be so fast so public? They are all war criminals in my view. What the outside world should be doing is giving them the message that, yes, other leaders should be allowed to emerge. Why didn't the US embassy also invite religious leaders, elders, women, professionals, when Aideed and Ali Mahdi met, to let these men know that these are the people they have stolen power from? It is a great pity they did not think of it. It sent all the wrong signals.[13]

In fact, this had been the strategy of Mohamed Sahnoun who was appointed UN Special Representative to Somalia in April 1992 and resigned in October because of frustration over UN policy. Sahnoun's role has become 'mythologised', to use Alex de Waal's word, in Somalia. He explicitly pursued what he called a 'civil society' strategy, including elders, women and neutral clans in a variety of talks: 'His strategy was not so much one of marginalizing the warlords as of including the non-warlords in political discussions.'[14]

The failure to take seriously alternative sources of power displays a myopia about the character of power and the relationship between power and violence. An effective response to the new wars has to be based on an alliance between international organizations and local advocates of cosmopolitanism in order to reconstruct legitimacy. A strategy of winning 'hearts and minds' needs to identify with individuals and groups respected for their integrity. They have to be supported, and their advice, proposals, recommendations need to be taken seriously. There is no standard formula for a cosmopolitan response; the point is rather that, in each local situation, there has to be a process involving these individuals and groups through which a strategy is developed. The various components of international involvement – the use of troops, the role of negotiation, funds for reconstruction – need to be worked out jointly.

This argument also has implications for the way in which political pressure from the above is exerted on political and military leaders to reach agreement or to consent to peacekeeping forces. Typical methods include the threat of air strikes or economic sanctions, which have the consequence of identifying the leaders with the population instead of isolating them, treating them as representative of 'sides', as legitimate leaders of states or proto-states. Such methods can easily be counterproductive, alienating the local population and narrowing the possibilities of pressure below. There may be circumstances in which these methods are an appropriate strategy and others where more targeted approaches may be more effective – arraigning the leaders as war criminals so that they cannot travel, exempting cultural communication so as to support civil society, for example. The point is that local cosmopolitans can provide the best advice on what is the best approach; they need to be consulted and treated as partners.

From Peacekeeping and / or Peace-enforcement to Cosmopolitan Law-enforcement

In the literature about peacekeeping, a rigid division tends to be drawn between peacekeeping and peace-enforcement.[15] Both terms are based on traditional assumptions about the character of war. Peacekeeping is based on the assumption that an agreement has been reached between the two sides in a war; the task of the peacekeeper is to supervise and monitor implementation of the agreement. The principles of peacekeeping as developed in the post-war period are consent, impartiality and the non-use of force. Peace-enforcement, on the other hand, which is authorized under Chapter VII of the UN Charter, is basically war-fighting; it means intervening in a war on one side. The distinction is considered important because war-fighting is assumed to involve the use of maximum force, since Clausewitzean wars tend to extremes. General Rose's preoccupation with 'Crossing the Mogadishu line' is about maintaining this distinction and not sliding from peacekeeping to peace-enforcement.

The analysis of new wars suggests that what is needed is not peacekeeping but enforcement of cosmopolitan norms, i.e. enforcement of international humanitarian and human rights law. Precisely because these wars are directed mainly against civilians, they do not have the same extremist logic as modern wars. Therefore, it ought to be possible to devise strategies for the protection of civilians and the capture of war criminals. The political aim is to provide secure areas in which alternative forms of inclusive politics can emerge. Many of the tactics that have been developed in recent wars are relevant – for example, the use of safety zones, humanitarian corridors, or no-fly zones – but their implementation up to now has been hampered by inflexible mandates and/or rigid adherence to what are viewed as the principles of peacekeeping. A number of authors have proposed new definitions for what is needed that fall between the perception of peacekeeping and peace-enforcement – such as 'second generation peacekeeping', 'robust peacekeeping', or the official British term 'wider peacekeeping' (which the British insist is still peacekeeping and not an in-between term) – but all of them tend to remain within the traditional framework of thinking about wars.[16]

Cosmopolitan law-enforcement is somewhere between soldiering and policing. Some of the tasks that international troops may be asked to perform fall within traditional ambits, for example, separating belligerents and maintaining ceasefires, controlling airspace. Others are essentially new tasks, e.g. the protection of safety zones or relief corridors. And yet others are close to traditional policing tasks – ensuring freedom of movement, guaranteeing the safety of individuals, especially returned refugees or displaced persons, and the capture of war criminals. Policing has been the great lacuna of peacekeeping. Back in the 1960s, when peacekeeping forces were sent to Cyprus, they were unable to prevent communal conflict because policing was not part of their mandate. Military forces have been notoriously unwilling to undertake police tasks, but, at the same time, it has proved difficult to recruit policemen because they are needed in their own societies. However one judges their record, the British forces in Northern Ireland did undertake policing tasks. Given the unlikelihood of another old war, military forces will eventually have to be reoriented to combine military and policing tasks.

Such tasks require enforcement and therefore necessarily involve the use of force, but in terms of the principles governing their application, the tasks of cosmopolitan law-enforcement are closer to peacekeeping. It is worth spelling out those principles and showing how they would need to be reformulated.

Consent

In the scenarios that were developed when preparing the official British peacekeeping manual, it was concluded that 'forcible pacification' is impracticable:

> Without the broader co-operation and consent of the majority of the local population and the leadership of the principal ruling authorities, be they parties to the dispute or government agencies, success is simply not a reasonable or realistic expectation. The risks entailed and force levels required of an approach that dispensed with a broad consensual framework is simply not a reasonable or realistic expectation. Put simply, consent (in its broadest form) is necessary for any prospect of success.[17]

According to this argument, consent is required at both the operational and the tactical level. At an operational level, consent is required before the mission is established. At a tactical level, commanders need to negotiate local consent.

The argument that 'forcible pacification' is impossible is clearly correct. The implication of the argument in this book is that international military forces have to be seen to be legitimate – that is to say, they have to operate on the basis of some sort of consent and even support, and to be acting within an agreed set of rules. Otherwise, there is a risk that they will become just another party to the conflict, as seems to have happened to some extent to the ECOMOG peacekeeping force in Liberia, where lack of pay, equipment and training meant that soldiers became engaged in the black market and/or theft from humanitarian supplies, and where the troops veered from neutrality to support for particular factions.[18]

However, unqualified consent is impossible; otherwise there would be no need for peacekeeping forces. If, for example, protection of humanitarian convoys is based on consent, then this can be negotiated as easily and perhaps more effectively by unarmed UN agencies or NGOs. The need for troops is based on the fact that not everyone consents and that those who prevent the convoys may have to be dealt with forcefully. For similar reasons, it may be impossible to obtain consent from *both* the local population and the warring parties. If an agreement has to be negotiated with a war criminal, then the credibility of the operation in the eyes of the local population may be damaged.

In general, international troops can expect considerable initial goodwill. In former Yugoslavia, the standing of the UN was very high; many local people had served in UN contingents. But the failure to react forcefully against those who interrupted aid convoys, to protect effectively safe havens, to capture war criminals or even maintain the No Fly Zone greatly undermined the legitimacy of the entire organization. The same was true in Somalia, where many local people hoped that the American troops who arrived in large numbers would disarm the warring parties. There was great disappointment when the Americans announced they would not disarm the factions and opened negotiations with the warlords. As a former Somali banker put it:

> You mean they have come all this way, with all this equipment and all these weapons just to move food from Baidoa to Berdara? (Laughter) Sooner rather than later, the fighting that continues in many parts of the country will displace people and create hunger and havoc in a few months. Then what? You can be sure there will not be more troops: Somalia, they will say, had its chance.[19]

What *is* important is widespread consent from the victims, the local population, whether or not formal consent has been obtained from the parties at an operational level. If consent at the operational level can be obtained, without sacrificing the goals of the mission, it is clearly an advantage. Retaining and building on the consent of the local population at a tactical level may well mean acting without the consent of one or other of the parties.

Impartiality

Impartiality tends to be interpreted as not taking sides. The ICRC makes a useful distinction between impartiality and neutrality. The principle of impartiality, it stated, means that it 'makes no discrimination as to nationality, race, religious beliefs, class, or political opinions. It endeavours to relieve the suffering of individuals, being guided solely by their needs, and to give priority to the most urgent cases of distress.' The principle of neutrality means that in 'order to continue to enjoy the confidence of all, the Red Cross may not take sides in hostilities or engage at any time in controversies of a political, racial, religious or ideological character'.[20]

In practice, impartiality and neutrality have been confused. The distinction is important for cosmopolitan law-enforcement. The law has to be enforced impartially, that is to say, without any discrimination on the basis of race, religion, etc. Since it is almost inevitable that one side violates the law more frequently than another, it is impossible to act according to both impartiality and neutrality. Neutrality may be important for an organization like the Red Cross which depends on consent for its activities, although the insistence on neutrality has frequently raised questions, particularly during World War II. It could also be important for the traditional concept of peacekeeping or for a purely humanitarian conception of the role of peacekeepers, i.e., the delivery of food. But if the task of the troops is to protect people and to stop violations of human rights, then insistence on neutrality is, at best, confusing and, at worst, undermines legitimacy.

According to Mackinlay: 'A UN soldier has the same approach as a policeman enforcing the law. He will uphold it regardless of which party is challenging him. But legitimacy must be intact at all levels.' However, Mackinlay seems to think that if the UN soldier enforces the rules impartially, it is possible to retain the respect of both sides.[21] The same point is made by Dobbie, one of the authors of the British peacekeeping manual, when he compares the role of the peacekeeper to the role of the referee at the football match. But these wars are not football matches; the various parties do not accept the rules. On the contrary, the nature of these wars is rule-breaking. The point is rather to persuade ordinary people of the advantages of rules so as to isolate and marginalize those who break them.

Use of Force

Traditional peacekeeping insisted on the non-use of force. The new British peacekeeping manual uses the term 'minimum necessary force', defined in the manual as 'the measured application of violence or coercion, sufficient only to achieve a specific end, demonstrably reasonable, proportionate and appropriate; and confined in effect to the specific and legitimate target intended.'[22]

The British contrast this position with what is known as the Weinberger/Powell doctrine of overwhelming force. The UN intervention in Somalia is often cited as an example of the perils of using force. It was largely an American intervention authorized under Chapter VII of the UN Charter. After an attack on Pakistani peacekeepers, the Americans began a manhunt for Mohammed Aideed. Bombardments in Southern Mogadishu resulted in many deaths and the manhunt for Aideed failed. (Owing to the refusal of the Americans to share intelligence information with the UN, a careful raid on what was supposed to be Aideed's hideout failed because it turned out to be a UN office.) The nadir for the Americans was reached when Aideed succeeded in shooting down two US helicopters killing eighteen soldiers, whose mutilated bodies were publicly paraded in front of television cameras, and wounding seventy-five others.

The problem, as various commentators have pointed out, was not the use of force as such, but the assumption of overwhelming force and the failure to take into account the local political situation and the need to act in such a way as to lend support to legitimacy and credibility. Ioan Lewis and James Mayall describe the American reaction to the initial killing of Pakistani peacekeepers:

> Instead of holding an independent legal enquiry and seeking to marginalize Aideed politically, Admiral Howe's forces reacted with injudicious force causing considerable Somali casualties – not necessarily all supporters of Aideed . . . Admiral Howe, behaving as if he were the Sheriff of Mogadishu, proclaimed Aideed an outlaw, offering a reward of $20,000 for his capture.[23]

Modern armies are uneasy about using minimum force because they are organized along Clausewitzean lines and have been trained to confront other similarly organized armies. As was shown in the case of Somalia, when confronted with the challenge of new wars, they find it extremely difficult to identify a middle way between the application of massive firepower and doing nothing. Unlike war-fighting, in which the aim is to maximize casualties on the other side and to minimize casualties on your own side, and peacekeeping, which does not use force, cosmopolitan law-enforcement has to minimize casualties on all sides. The significance of Nuremberg was that individuals and not collectivities were held responsible for war crimes. It is the arrest of individuals who may have committed war crimes or violations of human rights that is required for cosmopolitan law-enforcement, not the defeat of sides.

Cosmopolitan law-enforcement may mean risking the lives of peacekeepers in order to save the lives of victims. This is perhaps the most difficult presupposition to change. International personnel are always a privileged class in the new wars. The lives of UN or national personnel are valued over the lives of local people, despite the UN claim to be founded on the principles of humanity. The argument about humanitarian intervention revolves around whether it is acceptable to sacrifice national lives for the sake of people far away. The preference of Western powers, especially the United States, for air strikes, despite the physical and psychological damage caused even with highly accurate munitions, arises from this privileging of nationals or Westerners. This type of national or statist thinking has not yet come to terms with the concept of a common human community.

In effect, the proposal for cosmopolitan law-enforcement is an ambitious proposal to create a new kind of soldier-cum-policeman which will require considerable rethinking about tactics, equipment and, above all, command and training. The kind of equipment required is generally cheaper than that which national armed forces order for imagined Clausewitzean wars in the future. Transportation, especially air and sealift, is very important, as are efficient communications. Much of this equipment can be bought or rented from civilian sources, although military equipment tends to be more easily available and flexible. The American provision of airlift facilities has often been critical. In Bosnia and in Iraq, very sophisticated airborne equipment has been used in air strikes. While tactical air support and, indeed, air superiority may prove to be the decisive advantage of multinational peacekeeping forces in controlling violence, the utility of large-scale sophisticated air strikes is limited in relation to its disadvantages – collateral civilian damage, difficulty of hitting hidden targets, lack of control on the ground. Weapons that are heavier than those possessed by the warring parties may also prove important, although lack of manoeuvrability on difficult terrain may rule out many of the heavier types of equipment.

More importantly, the new cosmopolitan troops will have to be professionalized. Since they are likely to comprise multilateral forces, integrated command systems, joint exercises and standard rates of pay and conditions would need to be introduced. The new cosmopolitan troops have to become the legitimate bearers of arms. They have to know and respect the laws of war and follow a strict code of conduct. Reports of corruption or violations of human rights have to be properly investigated.[24] Above all, the motivations of these new forces have to be incorporated into a wider concept of cosmopolitan right. Whereas the soldier, as the legitimate bearer of arms, had to be prepared to die for his country, the international soldier/policeman risks his or her life for humanity.

From Humanitarian Assistance to Reconstruction

Mark Duffield writes about a two-tier system of economic assistance in the 1990s. On the one hand, official assistance is predicated on structural adjustment programmes or transition strategies which contribute to the decline of the formal economy. On the other hand, a safety net to cope with the consequences has been developed, largely based on contracting out the provision of assistance to NGOs.[25] A similar point is made by Alvaro de Soto and Graciana del Castillo in their discussion of the lack of coordination between the IMF and the World Bank, on the one hand, and the UN, on the other. The consequences and the cost in political and humanitarian terms of the policies of the former agencies are simply not taken into account. They describe the problems of implementing a peace programme in El Salvador against the backdrop of an IMF stabilization programme. In order to keep within the IMF spending limits, El Salvador was unable to afford to build a national civil police force and to embark on an arms-for-land programme to reintegrate guerrillas as required by the peace agreement: 'The adjustment program and the stabilization plan, on the one hand, and the peace process, on the other, were born and reared as if they were children of different families. They lived under different roofs. They had little in common other than belonging roughly to the same generation.'[26]

During the 1990s, there has been a big increase in humanitarian assistance; nowadays it amounts to over 10 per cent of official development assistance. The establishment of the UN Department of Humanitarian Affairs in 1991 and of the European Community Humanitarian Office (ECHO) in 1992 reflects the growing importance of humanitarian assistance. In chapter 5 I described the way in which the provision of humanitarian assistance is built into the functioning of the war economy. In fact, humanitarian assistance also contributes to the failures of the formal economy. It substitutes for local production. In Somalia, the policy of flooding the country with food in late 1992 in order to ensure that some aid reached those who really needed food led to a dramatic fall in prices, so that it was no longer economical for farmers to produce food.[27] In Tuzla, a centre of salt-mining, several tons of salt were being thrown away every day because it was dangerous to halt mining, yet UNHCR was importing salt from the Netherlands for humanitarian purposes. Humanitarian programmes also tend to bypass local specialists and create new hierarchies, in which those who work for international agencies receive salaries and other perks, while well-qualified local people, like doctors and teachers, live off humanitarian aid.

Humanitarian assistance is essential; otherwise, people would starve. But it needs to be much more carefully targeted, taking the advice of local experts who really know the local situation. And it needs to be accompanied by assistance for reconstruction. By reconstruction, I mean the rebuilding of a formal political economy, based on accepted rules, and the reversal of the negative social and economic relationships I described in chapter 5. The word 'reconstruction' has other connotations drawn from earlier wars. It is usually assumed to be a programme of economic assistance, on the 1947 Marshall Plan model, that is put into effect once an overall political settlement has been reached. Aid agencies often insist that no reconstruction assistance can be provided before a political settlement is reached and, indeed, that the lure of reconstruction assistance represents an incentive to reach a political settlement. But I have argued that a lasting settlement can only be reached in a situation based on alternative politics, the politics of civility – which is very difficult so long as these negative social and economic relations persist. Instead, reconstruction should be viewed as a strategy to achieve peace rather than a strategy for after peace has been established.

The situation in what might be called near war economies is not so very different from situations of war. Whether we are referring to places where ceasefires have recently been agreed to or to 'bad neighbourhoods' where the negative relationships of war have spread, the symptoms are much the same – unemployment, breakdown of basic infrastructure, pervasive criminality – and these are the symptoms that contribute to the outbreak or renewal of war. In other words, reconstruction is both a pre-war and a post-war strategy, aimed at prevention and at cure.

Reconstruction has to mean, first and foremost, the rebuilding of political authorities, even if only at the local level, and the reconstruction of civil society in the sense both of law and order and of providing the conditions in which alternative political groupings can mobilize. It does not mean reconstruction of what went before. Necessarily, it must entail the restructuring of political and economic arrangements so as not to repeat the conditions that gave rise to war. The adaptation of appropriate forms of governance and the introduction of regulated market relationships take time, and have to be part of a long-term process through which different groups in society can participate.

It is often argued that reconstruction has to encompass transition, in the sense that there is clearly a need to reform the institutions that preceded the war. Unfortunately, the term transition has come to be associated with a standard formula for democratization and transition to the market, which includes the formal aspects of democracy, for example elections, as well as economic liberalization and privatization. In the absence of meaningful political institutions through which genuine debate and participation can take place, and in situations where the rule of law is weak and where trust and confidence is lacking, this standard formula can exacerbate the underlying problems, providing incentives for exclusivist politics or for criminalization of formerly state-owned enterprises. Reconstruction has to involve reform, but not necessarily along the lines of the standard transition formula

Reconstruction should be focused on zones of civility so that they can act as models encouraging similar initiatives in other places. Where legitimate local authorities do not exist, local trusteeships or protectorates could be proposed. The experience of the EU administration in Mostar has led to scepticism about the idea of local trusteeships. The problem there, however, was that the administration did not have adequate policing capacities and had to share power with the nationalist parties which controlled the police forces and included notorious criminals. The rhetoric of self-help is used as an argument against trusteeships or protectorates, but it is very difficult for people to help themselves when they are at the mercy of gangsters.

The primary requisite is the restoration of law and order in order to create a situation in which normal life can resume and refugees and displaced persons can be repatriated. This task includes disarmament, demobilization, protection of the area, capture of war criminals, policing and/or establishing and training local police forces, and the restoration of the judiciary.

Mats Berdal has shown that the record of efforts at achieving disarmament and demobilization has been poor.[28] It is very difficult for UN forces to achieve more than partial disarmament and techniques like weapons 'buy-back' programmes have tended to result in the handing back of sub-standard weapons, while the high-quality weapons remain hidden. Moreover, there are now so many sources for acquisition, at least of small arms, both because of the high number of producers and the availability of surplus weapons, that the task is never-ending. Creating a secure environment may well turn out to be more important than disarmament. Effective policing and the capture of war criminals are essential conditions for security, whether they are undertaken by international forces, together with civilian affairs officers, local police forces under international supervision, or whether local authorities can take responsibility, perhaps with some outside support, as is the case in better-established zones of civility.

As well as disarmament and policing, law and order needs an independent and trustworthy judiciary and an active civil society, i.e. the creation of a relatively free public space. For this reason, investment in education and a free media are essential to stop the relentless particularistic propaganda and to end not just physical intimidation but also psychological intimidation. These conditions are much more important than the formal procedures of democracy. Outsiders often insist on elections as a way of providing a timetable and terminal point for their involvement.

But without the preconditions of security, public space, reconciliation and open dialogue, elections may end up legitimizing
the warring parties, as was the case, for example, in Bosnia after
Dayton.

To create a self-sustaining zone of civility, so that law and
order, education and media can be paid for, so that soldiers find
jobs and education, and taxes are paid, the local economy has to
be restored. As well as disarmament, demobilization is also difficult, and not only because of the insecure environment. Many
soldiers would like to give up banditry and find settled jobs or,
in the case of children and young people, an education. But demobilization programmes have not been very successful because
of unemployment and labour shortages, and inadequate educa-
tional facilities.

The priorities are basic services and local production. Infrastructure – water, power, transport, post and telecommunica-
tions – needs to be restored at both local and regional levels. As
well as being necessary on grounds of need, infrastructure is vital for the restoration of normal trade links and can be a subject
of negotiation even when there is no agreement in other areas.
Even at the height of wars, it is sometimes possible to reach
agreement on these kinds of concrete issue, especially where
there is a mutual interest. Gas supplies to Sarajevo were maintained more or less throughout the war, for example. The other
area is support for local production of basic necessities so as to
reduce the need for humanitarian assistance, especially food,
clothing, building materials and so on. Along with public services, this is a good way to generate local employment.

In so far as reconstruction is a strategy for peace, it has to
provide economic security and hope for the future so as to remove the atmosphere of fear in which people live, and to offer,
young people especially, an alternative livelihood to the army or
the mafia. What needs to be done is specific in every situation
but certain principles can be specified.

First, all assistance projects should be based on the principles
of openness and integration. It is all too easy, in the interests of
restoring services, to accept divisions and partitions established
through war and, thereby, legitimize the status quo instead of
helping to change it. In Mostar, for example, the EU Administration was supposed to reintegrate the town, which was divided
between a Croat and a Muslim half. Although in a few limited

cases, for example water supply, the EU managed to negotiate common projects, for the most part it has turned out to be easier to introduce separate projects in each half of the town, thereby explicitly following a strategy of separate development. Because there was no secure environment and because the EU feared taking sides, everything had to be negotiated between the nationalist leaders. Openness and integration means that anyone should be able to benefit from the projects and that projects are explicitly directed towards bringing people together, through, for example, employing refugees, displaced persons or demobilized soldiers, or involving an element of sharing. Openness and integration need to be fostered not only at a local level, but also at national and regional levels.

Second, assistance needs to be decentralized and to encourage local initiatives. By spreading recipients, more people are involved in the programme, there are greater possibilities for experiment and there is less risk of aid being creamed off or being distorted by political compromises. Where demobilization has taken place, it has been local community-based programmes, often organized by the veterans themselves, which seem to have been the most successful – for example, the Uganda Veterans' Board or the National Demobilization Commission in Somaliland, which developed a programme of demobilization and reintegration together with the veterans' organization SOYAAL. Some veterans explained:

> The boys on the 'technicals' (pick-up vehicles mounted with machine guns or anti-tank guns) are themselves tired. They see no benefit, only death. They climb the technicals out of need. Some of those in secure jobs now include some who were the worst gangsters. They prefer the $200 that comes with a settled job to the millions they get as bandits.[29]

Third, it is very important to make use of local specialists and to encourage a wide-ranging local debate about how aid should be provided. This is important in order to increase efficiency by using people who have knowledge and experience of the area, to increase transparency, to reduce corruption and to build up civic engagement.

Even in areas that seem the most intractable there are some possibilities for funding this type of assistance. The strategy of expanding zones of civility to offset the spread of 'bad neigh-bourhoods' needs to be able to extend itself directly into the bad neighbourhoods. Poor, uncivil areas become caught in a vicious circle in which assistance is refused because of the behaviour of the local 'authorities'; unemployment and criminality flourish, thereby helping to sustain the position of the particularist war-lords. It is all the more important to identify ways to support certain bottom-up projects that cross war divides in order to begin to open up spaces in these areas.

Reconstruction can be thought of as a new approach to devel-opment, an alternative to both structural adjustment/transition and humanitarianism. As is the case of cosmopolitan law-en-forcement, it is bound to be costly in the short term, to require greater resources than rich countries have so far been willing to commit to peacekeeping and overseas assistance. It would mean abandoning some of the neo-liberal assumptions about levels of public expenditure that have dominated international economic orthodoxy in recent years. Reconstruction means that politics, economics and security issues have to be integrated into a new type of humanistic global policy which should be capable of enhancing the legitimacy of international institutions and mobi-lizing popular support.

7

Governance, Legitimacy and Security

Liberal writers of the late eighteenth and nineteenth centuries had a teleological view of history. They believed that the zone of civility would, inevitably, extend itself in time and space. In his book *Reflections on Violence*,[1] John Keane contrasts their optimism with the pessimism of twentieth-century writers like Zygmunt Bauman or Norbert Elias, who considered that barbarism was the inevitable concomitant of civility. For these writers, violence is embedded in human nature. The cost of allowing the state to monopolize violence is the terrible barbarity of twentieth-century wars and totalitarianism.

The end of the Cold War may mark the end of statist barbarism on this scale. Certainly, the threat of modern war and, in particular, the threat of nuclear war – the absolute expression of twentieth-century barbarism – have receded. Does this mean that violence can no longer be controlled, that the new type of warfare described in the previous chapters is likely to be pervasive, an ongoing characteristic of the post-modern world? The implication of the argument so far is that it is no longer possible to contain war geographically. Zones of peace and zones of war exist side by side in the same territorial space. The characteristics of the new wars I have described – the politics of identity, the decentralization of violence, the globalized war economy – can be found in greater or lesser degree all over the world. Moreover, through transnational criminal networks, diaspora networks based on identity, the explosive growth of refugees and asylum-seekers, as well as the global media, these characteristics have a tendency to spread. The gang warfare of inner cities in the North, conflicts in places like Bosnia and Somalia and even the virtual old-style wars conducted through air strikes are all manifestations of the new types of organized violence.

But if it is not possible to contain the new wars territorially, is it possible to envisage ways in which they might be contained politically? Globalization, after all, is a process which involves integration and inclusion as well as fragmentation and exclusivism. A new cosmopolitan politics, based on goals such as peace, human rights or environmentalism, is emerging side by side with the politics of particularism. Are the pessimists right? Is violence inherent in human society? Or could the new cosmopolitan politics offer a basis for restoring legitimacy at both local and global levels? Can we conceive of a world in which violence is controlled on a transnational scale, in which the monopoly of legitimate violence is reclaimed by global or transnational institutions, and in which the abuse of power by those same institutions can be checked by an alert and active cosmopolitan citizenry?

As I argued in chapter 2, military power in the post-war period was to a large degree transnationalized. The rigidification of the alliances in Europe and the establishment of integrated command systems, together with a global network of military connections through military assistance, arms sales and training, effectively meant that most countries, apart from the superpowers, abandoned the unilateral capacity to wage wars. Although there has been some re-nationalization of armed forces in the aftermath of the Cold War, there has also been a whole set of new arrangements – multinational peace-keeping, arms-control agreements involving mutual inspection teams, joint exercises, new or renewed organizations like the WEU, Partnership for Peace, NATO Coordination Council (NACC) – which constitute an intensification of trans-nationalization in the military sphere. During the Cold War, the boundaries of violence were extended to the edges of the two blocs; or, to put it another way, pacification was achieved throughout the bloc system. The question is whether this transnational agglomeration of military power can lead to global pacification. Can we conceive of pacification without territorial boundaries?

There is no self-evident answer. In every era there is a complex relationship between processes of governance (how human affairs are managed), legitimacy (on which the power to govern is based) and forms of security (how organized violence is controlled). On the one hand, the ability to maintain order, to protect individuals in a physical sense, to provide a secure basis for administrative capacities, to guarantee the rule of law and to protect territory externally are all primary functions of political institutions from which they derive legitimacy. Moreover, the character of these institutions is largely defined in relation to the way in which these functions are undertaken and which aspects of security are accorded priority. On the other hand, it is not possible to provide security in the sense defined above without some underlying legitimacy. There has to be some mechanism, whether it is religious injunction, ideological fanaticism or democratic consent, which explains why people obey rules and why, in particular, agents of organized violence – soldiers or policemen, for example – follow orders.

In chapter 2, I described the way in which the evolution of modern (old) war was linked to the emergence of the European nation-state, in which internal pacification was associated with the externalization of violence and legitimacy derived from notions of patriotism embedded in the actual experience of war. The term 'national security' was largely synonymous with external defence of national borders. In the post-war period, the internal / external distinction extended to bloc boundaries, and ideological identities – notions of freedom and/or socialism – drawn from the experience of the Second World War supplanted but did not displace national identities as a basis for bloc legitimacy. Bloc security also meant external defence of the blocs.

Today, there is great uncertainty about future patterns of governance. There is talk of a 'security vacuum'. The debate about how to fill that vacuum is largely an institutional debate. In Europe, it revolves around the future of NATO and the role of other European institutions such as the WEU, OSCE, the CIS and so on. But underlying the institutional debate is a real set of questions about the control of violence. The national monopoly of legitimate organized violence has been eroded from above by the transnationalization of military forces. It has been eroded from below by the privatization of organized violence which is characteristic of the new wars. Under what conditions are existing or new security institutions able to eliminate or marginalize privatized forms of violence?

My argument is that this depends on political choice and how we choose to analyse the nature of contemporary violence and what conception of security we adopt. Traditional political science rooted in nineteenth- and twentieth-century experience is only able to predict a new variant of the past or else the descent into chaos. Precisely because the dominant stream of political science thinking was directed towards the existing system of governance, providing at once a form of justification or legitimation of that system and at the same time a basis for offering advice about how to operate within the system, it gives rise to a kind of fatalism or determinism about the future. In contrast, critical or normative approaches to political science allow for human agency. They are based on the assumption that people make their own history and can choose their futures, at least within a certain framework that can be analysed.

In what follows, I outline some possible ways of thinking about security which derive from competing political visions of the future based on differing perceptions of the nature of contemporary violence. One of these visions is a restoration of world order based on the reconstruction of some kind of bloc system in which cleavages based on identity supplant cleavages based on ideology. This approach draws on realist assumptions about international relations in which the main actors are territorially-based political authorities and new wars are treated as a variant of old wars – geo-political conflicts. The most well-known example of this type of thinking is in Samuel Huntington's *Clash of Civilizations*, where he proposes a variant of the bloc system based on cultural identity instead of ideology.[2] A second vision can be described as neo-medievalism[3] or as anarchy, and draws on a post-modern rejection of realism.[4] Proponents of this line of thought recognize that the new wars cannot be understood in old terms, but at the same time are unable to identify any logic in the new wars. They are treated as a Hobbesian 'warre' against all.[5] This vision is, essentially, a counsel of despair, an admission of our inability to analyse global developments. Finally, a third vision is based on a more normative approach, drawing on the argument put forward for cosmopolitanism in the previous chapter.

The Clash of Civilizations

Huntington's thesis is a variant of the bloc system in which the source of legitimacy is cultural identity – loyalty to what he defines as historic civilizations. His book has received so much attention because it expresses what many believe to be the unstated convictions of parts of the political establishment, particularly those whose livelihood depended on the Cold War – an attempt to recreate the comfortable certainties of the bipolar world and to construct a new threat to substitute for communism. The Gulf War represented the paradigm for Huntington's approach; Saddam Hussein was literally built up in the communist image. The plan rolled out by the Pentagon had originally been designed to contain a Soviet thrust southwards towards the Persian Gulf. By following organizational routine and mobilizing on a scale commensurate with a Cold War scenario, Saddam Hussein was transformed into a formidable enemy equivalent to his Soviet predecessor.[6]

Huntington argues that we are entering a multi-civilizational world in which culture rather than ideology will be the bonding mechanism for societies and groups of states. As many critics have pointed out, he is rather vague about what is meant by culture, although clearly, for him, religion is a key defining element. Thus, the West is Christian, but only Catholic and Protestant. He is adamant that Turkey cannot be allowed to join the EU because it is Muslim, and he considers that the membership of Greece, an Orthodox country, is a mistake; according to Huntington, Greece is definitely not part of Western civilization. It is also clear that, for him, states are the key guarantors of civilizations. He emphasizes the role of 'core states', e.g. the USA for the West and China for Asia.

He defines some six or seven civilizations (Sinic, Japanese, Hindu, Islamic, Western, Latin American and, possibly, African). But he sees the dominant cleavage which shapes global order running between the West and either Islam or Asia. Islam is viewed as a threat because of population growth and what he sees as the Muslim 'propensity for violence'. Asia is viewed as a threat because of rapid economic growth organized around what he calls the 'bamboo network' of ethnic Chinese. For Huntington, the West is defined as American political creed plus Western culture. He takes the view that Western culture is decaying and must defend itself against alien cultures; in particular, the USA and Europe must stick together as they did in the Cold War period.

The main source of violence comes from what Huntington calls 'fault-line wars'. He argues that communal conflicts are a fact of contemporary existence; in other words, he accepts the primordialist conception of the new conflicts. According to him, they are increasing in scale partly because of the collapse of communism and partly because of demographic changes. (He thinks that the war in Bosnia was mainly a consequence of the higher birth rate of Muslims.) When communal conflicts involve different civilizations, as in Bosnia–Herzegovina, they become fault-line wars, calling into being what he calls the kin-country syndrome. Hence, Russia was brought into the Bosnian conflict on the Serbian side, Germany on the Croatian side and the Islamic states on the Bosnian side. (He is a little puzzled by US support for Bosnia, which does not quite fit the thesis, but it can be explained away in terms of the mistaken legacy of a universalizing political ideology.) In other words, the new wars are to be subsumed into a dominant civilizational clash and superpower patrons are to be re-created on a cultural rather than an ideological basis.

Huntington is, at once, highly critical of a global universalizing mission, describing himself as a cultural relativist, and, at the same time, deeply opposed to multiculturalism. He argues that the USA no longer has the capacity to act as a global power, citing the overstretch of US forces at the time of the Gulf War, and that its task is to protect Western civilization in a multi-civilizational world. He also considers that human rights and individualism are purely Western phenomena and we have no right to impose Western political values on societies to whom this is alien. At the same time, he argues that the USA has the task of preserving Western culture domestically. Hence, what he envisages is a kind of global apartheid in which relatively homogeneous civilizations held together from above by core states become mutual guardians of international order, helping each other through their mutual confrontation to preserve the purity of their respective civilizations. In other words, he is proposing a form of bloc political mobilization based on exclusive identity: 'In the greater clash, the global "real clash" between

Civilization and barbarism, the world's great civilizations . . . will . . . hang together or hang separately. In the emerging era, clashes of civilization are the greatest threat to world peace, and an international order based on civilizations is the surest safeguard against world war.'[7]

A major problem for Huntington is the fact that the Muslim world has no core state capable of keeping order. Just as the USA needed the Soviet Union to sustain the bipolar order of the Cold War years, so the Huntington scenario requires a stable enemy. The absence of a core Muslim state is more than just a problem for the argument, for it has something to do with the fragility of the entire theoretical framework. For Huntington, it is geo-politics as usual. In his framework, states retain the monopoly of legitimate organized violence. Civilizational security is provided by core states and, at least implicitly, provides the basis for the legitimacy of civilizational blocs. But is this realistic?

Huntington does not ask why the Soviet Union collapsed nor what are the factors that characterize the current transition period. Words like 'globalization' or 'civil society' simply do not enter the Huntington vocabulary. For him, history is about changing state relations; models of state structures can be constructed without any regard to changing state–society relations. Seemingly random developments like population growth or urbanization are invoked to explain particular phenomena such as the growth of fundamentalism or the strength of China. But there is no questioning of the content of governance, of how political institutions change in character, and little explanation about how the world moves from today's uncertainty to the new civilizational order. It is assumed that territorial defence of civilizations is the way to maintain order; it ignores the complexities of forms of violence which are neither internal nor external, public nor private.

Nevertheless, the Huntington thesis is influential. I have explored the argument at length because elements of Huntington's thinking are implicit in the security debate of the late 1990s, especially in Europe, even if they are expressed in less extreme ways. Hence, the debate about the enlargement of the EU and NATO and about where Europe ends is not conducted in terms of real security needs, but, rather, in terms of which countries are 'eligible' (worthy) to be members of these institutions. According to this approach, Europe has a territorial boundary and certain criteria (levels of income, levels of democratic performance) are used to decide which countries fall inside the boundary. Thus, President Václav Havel, keen that the Czech Republic should join NATO, has talked of a Euro-Atlantic Community of like-minded nations, while the European Christian Democrats have publicly expressed their view that Turkey should not join the EU because it is a Muslim country.

The Coming Anarchy

In contrast to Huntington's thesis, the strength of the anarchy argument is that it takes account of the break with the past and the difference between old and new wars. Robert D. Kaplan's book *The Ends of the Earth: A Journey at the Dawn of the Twenty First Century* is a good example of this type of thinking. It is a kind of political travel book, which contains compelling descriptions of social life as it exists today on the ground. His conclusions are thus derived from direct experience of contemporary realities. Kaplan draws attention to the erosion of state authority in many parts of the world and the myopia induced by a state-centric view of the world:

> What if there are really not fifty-odd nations in Africa as the maps suggest – what if there are only six, or seven, or eight real nations on the continent? Or, instead of nations, several hundred tribal entities? . . . What if the territory held by guerrilla armies and urban mafias – territory that is never shown on maps – is more significant than the territory claimed by many recognized states? What if Africa is even further away from North America and Europe than the maps indicate?[8]

In Sierra Leone, he discovers the breakdown of the monopoly of organized violence, the weakening of the distinction between 'armies and civilians, and armies and criminal gangs'.[9] In Pakistan, he discovers a 'decomposing polity based more on criminal activities than effective government'.[10] In Iran, he speculates about a new type of economy based on the bazaar. His journey gives him scope to describe the growing scarcity of resources, widespread environmental degradation, the pressures of urbanization and the new class of restless, unemployed young urban dwellers attracted to the certainties of religious fundamentalism. He talks about global inequalities of wealth and about the global communications revolution which has made these disparities so visible. He describes the growth of NGOs as 'the international army of the future'.[11] He dwells on the impact of modern technology on traditional societies – the radio, for example, as magic in Africa.

In his original article in *The Atlantic Monthly*, Kaplan coined the phrase the 'coming anarchy' to depict a world in which civil order had broken down. In West Africa, he observed a return to nature and to Hobbesian chaos which he argued prefigured the future elsewhere in the world. Referring to Africa, Kaplan told a BBC interviewer in March 1995:

> You have a lot of people in London and Washington who fly all over the world, who stay in luxury hotels, who think that English is dominating every place, but yet they have no idea what is out there. Out there is that thin membrane of luxury hotels, of things that work, of civil order, which is proportionately getting thinner and thinner and thinner.[12]

In his book, the thesis is somewhat modified. He also finds islands of civility, in Eritrea, in Risha valley in India, or in the slums of Istanbul, where local people have succeeded in establishing or maintaining new or traditional forms of self-management. He is doubtful about whether these relatively isolated examples can provide models for other regions, arguing that their success largely depends on whether or not they have inherited certain civic-minded traditions, on what is or is not inherent in local culture. He goes on to argue:

> The map of the world will never be static. The future map – in a sense, the 'last map' – will be an ever-mutating representation of cartographic chaos: in some areas benign, or even productive, and in some areas violent. Because the map will be always changing, it may be updated, like weather reports, and transmitted daily over the internet in those places that have reliable electricity or private generators. On this map, the rules by which diplomats and other policymaking elites have ordered the world these past few hundred years will apply less and less. Solutions in the main, will have to come from within the affected cultures themselves.[13]

Kaplan's argument is essentially determinist. While he rightly dismisses geo-political solutions of the Huntington type drawn on the state-centric assumptions of the past, he implicitly shares Huntington's assumption that the prospects for governance depend on essentialist assumptions about culture. Because he witnesses collapsing states and because he cannot envisage alternative forms of authority at a global level, his scenario contains no security and no legitimacy except in certain arbitrary instances. Like Huntington, Kaplan laments the passing of the Cold War, suggesting that we may, in future, come to see it as an interlude between violence and chaos, like the Golden Age of Athenian democracy. He concludes his book with an admission of helplessness: 'I would be unfaithful to my experience if I thought we had a general solution to these problems. We are not in control. As societies grow more populous and complex, the idea that a global elite like the UN can engineer reality from above is just as absurd as the idea that political "science" can reduce any of this to a science.'[14]

Cosmopolitan Governance

In contrast to the above approaches, the project for cosmopolitan governance, or humane governance as Richard Falk calls it,[15] breaks with the assumption of territorially-based political entities. It is a project which derives from a humanist universalist outlook and which crosses the global/local divide. It is based on an alliance, as described in the previous chapter, between islands of civility, noted by Kaplan, and transnational institutions. There are no boundaries in a territorial sense. But there are political boundaries – between those who support cosmopolitan civic values, who favour openness, toleration and participation, on the one hand, and those who are tied to particularist, exclusivist, often collectivist political positions, on the other. In the nineteenth century, the dominant international cleavages were national, tied to a territorial definition of nation. These were replaced in the twentieth century by ideological cleavages between left and right or between democracy/capitalism and socialism, which also became tied to territory. The cleavage between cosmopolitanism and particularisms cannot be territorially defined, even though every individual particularism makes its own territorial claim.

This is not a project for a single world government. The Kantian notion of cosmopolitan right was based on the assumption of a federation of sovereign states; cosmopolitan right was essentially a set of rules agreed by all the members of the federation. Essentially, what is proposed is a form of 'global overwatch'. It is possible to envisage a range of territorially-based political entities, from municipalities to nation-states to continental organizations, which operate within a set of accepted rules, standards of international behaviour. The job of international institutions is to ensure implementation of those rules, particularly as regards human rights and humanitarian law. Just as it is increasingly accepted that governments can intervene in family affairs to stop domestic violence, so a similar principle would be applied on a global scale.

In some senses, a cosmopolitan regime already exists.[16] Transnational NGOs monitor and draw public attention to abuses of human rights, to genocide and other war crimes, and international institutions do respond in different ways. What has been lacking up to now has been enforcement. The argument here is that some form of cosmopolitan law-enforcement, as elaborated in the previous chapter, would underpin a cosmopolitan regime. In effect, it would fill the security vacuum and enhance the legitimacy of international institutions, enabling them to mobilize public support and to act in other fields, for example, the environment or poverty. Of course, international institutions would need to increase their accountability and transparency, to develop democratic procedures for authorizing the use of legitimate force. What this might entail is outside the scope of this book.[17] The point is, rather, that just as the development of the modern state involved a symbiotic process through which war, administrative structures and legitimacy evolved, so the development of cosmopolitan governance and, indeed, democracy is already taking place through a similar although evidently fragile process involving growing administrative responsibility for upholding cosmopolitan norms.

What are the implications of this approach for the debate about European security? Any security organization has to be inclusive rather than exclusive. An organization with boundaries is one which implicitly emphasizes external defence against a common enemy rather than cosmopolitan law-enforcement. The advantage of NATO was that it became the instrument through which military forces were transnationalized; it provided a basis for transnational pacification. This is probably the most important reason why a war between France and Germany is now unthinkable. The disadvantage was that it kept alive the prospect of bloc war. The proposed enlargement of NATO will include Hungary but not Romania, the Czech Republic but not Slovakia, Poland but not most of the former Soviet Union. External defence of NATO will not protect NATO countries from the spread of new wars, but it will treat those countries outside the boundaries as potential enemies. Those countries that are poorer with less well-established political institutions, that are perhaps Muslim and/or Orthodox, are designated as outsiders. This is unlikely to create a new civilizational order on the Huntingtonian model. On the contrary, exclusion is likely to contribute to the conditions that give rise to the new type of warfare which could easily spread.

A cosmopolitan approach to European and, indeed, global security would try to bring together potentially conflicting countries and to spread as far as possible the transnationalization of armed forces. This could be under the umbrella of NATO, including Russia, the OSCE, or the United Nations. The important point is not the name of the organization but how the security task is reconceptualized. A cosmopolitan approach to security, encompasses political and economic approaches to security, as described in chapter 6. The task of the agents of legitimate organized violence, under the umbrella of transnational institutions, is not external defence as was the case for national or bloc models of security, but cosmopolitan law-enforcement.

Conclusion

Table 7.1 provides a schematic description of the relationship between patterns of governance and forms of security and how this relationship would vary according to the competing visions I have described.

Which of the last three scenarios – clash of civilizations, coming anarchy, cosmopolitan governance – will the future hold?

Table 7.1   *Patterns of governance*

Patterns of governance	Political institutions	Source of legitimacy	Mode of security
States system	Nation-states	Nation-building, patriotism	External defence, internal pacification
Cold War	Nation-states, blocs, transnational institutions	Ideology – freedom or socialism	Deterrence, bloc cohesion
Clash of civilizations	Nation-states, civilizational blocs	Cultural identity	Civilizational defence at home and abroad
Coming anarchy	Pockets of authority	Non-existent	Fortified islands of civility amidst pervasive violence
Cosmopolitan governance	Transnational institutions, nation-states, local government	Humanism	End of modern war, cosmopolitan law-enforcement

Prediction is not possible. The answer depends on the outcome of public debates, on the responses of institutions, on political choices being made at various levels of society. The future may turn on what happens in Bosnia. In the late 1990s there are 30,000 troops in Bosnia involving NATO, Partnership for Peace countries and others. With the exception of Russian troops, they operate under a NATO command, authorized by the UN and, as I pointed out in chapter 3, the operation is the largest military deployment outside the NATO area ever to have been undertaken by the organization. Bosnia may be to the post-Cold War period what Germany was for the post-war period – a paradigm for our competing conceptions of security.

All three approaches I have described are contending in Bosnia–Herzegovina. There are those who see the operation as Huntington-style action. The troops are presiding over the partition of Bosnia between a Catholic part and an Orthodox part and maybe a Muslim part as well. Croatia and Slovenia, together with the Catholic part of Bosnia, will become part of a new Euro-Atlantic bloc. Serbia and the Muslim rump will be abandoned to the 'backward East' on the side of Russia. There are those, especially in the US Congress, who consider that the whole operation is a great waste of money; they favour withdrawal as soon as possible. They are ready to accept anarchy or chaos in places far away and believe that it is possible to fortify themselves against its spread. And there are those in Bosnia as well as outside, among local NGOs as well as international institutions, who are struggling to integrate Bosnia as well as the outside forces, who favour the capture of war criminals, the control of police forces, the establishment of a free pluralistic media and multicultural education, and the reconstruction of economic and social relationships.

Critics of the cosmopolitan approach might argue that it is a modernist / universalist project on an even more ambitious scale than earlier modernist projects like liberalism or socialism, and thus contains within it a totalitarian claim. Moreover, given the secular character of the concept and the explicit rejection of identity-based forms of communitarianism, it might be argued that the concept is open to more severe charges of utopianism and inconsistency than were earlier modernist projects. I take the view that public morality has to be underpinned by universalist projects, although those projects are periodically changed by circumstances; they always produce unintended consequences and have to be revised. Thus, they can never be universalistic in practice, even if they make universalistic claims. Such projects, like liberalism or socialism, are validated by circumstances, at least for a time, or discredited. The eighteenth-century idea that reason is immanent in nature implied that rational (moral) behaviour can be learned through experience; there is a reality in which there are better or worse ways of living and that how to live in these different ways can be learned through experience, for example, the experience of happy or unhappy families or of war and peace. These lessons are never learned for ever because reality is so complicated and the exact set of circumstances in which a particular rationality seems to work cannot be reproduced. But they can be learned for a while and in approximate circumstances.

In today's reflexive era, a cosmopolitan project is, of its nature, tentative. We are likely to live permanently with contending approaches, although the character and assumptions of the different approaches are bound to keep changing. It may be that no approach will dominate in Bosnia, but the operation in Bosnia may well represent for some time to come a new narrative, a way of telling the story of our political differences.

The optimistic view of current developments is the obsolescence of modern war. War, as we have known it for the last two centuries, may, like slavery, have become an anachronism. National armies, navies and airforces may be no more than ritual vestiges of the passing nation-state. 'Perpetual Peace', as envisaged by Immanuel Kant, the globalization of civility, the development of cosmopolitan forms of governance are real possibilities. The pessimistic view is that war, like slavery, can always be reinvented. The capacity of formal political institutions, primarily nation-states, to regulate violence has been eroded and we have entered an era of long-term low-level informal violence, of post-modern warfare. In this book, I have argued that both views are correct. We cannot assume that either barbarism or civility is embedded in human nature. Whether we can learn to cope with the new wars and veer towards a more optimistic future depends ultimately on our own behaviour.

Afterword

This book was published just before the Nato bombing campaign against Yugoslavia in 1999. Subsequently, I became a member of the Independent International Commission on Kosovo (IICK) and had the opportunity to collect evidence and engage in intensive discussions about what happened in Kosovo.[1] As 'new wars' continue to spread, with continuing conflicts in places such as Sierra Leone, Chechnya, Palestine or Kashmir, it is all the more important to reflect on the implications of the Kosovo crisis for our understanding of this type of war and the international responses.

The intervention in Kosovo was hailed as the first war for human rights. The British Prime Minister, Tony Blair, used the occasion of NATO's fiftieth anniversary, which took place during the air strikes, to enunciate a new 'Doctrine of International Community'. 'We are all internationalists now whether we like it or not,' he told an audience in Chicago. 'We cannot refuse to participate in global markets if we want to prosper. We cannot ignore new political ideas in other countries if we want to innovate. We cannot turn our backs on conflicts and the violation of human rights in other countries if we still want to be secure.'[2]

But the actual record of the war is much more ambiguous. The proclaimed goal did represent an innovation and an important precedent in international behaviour; it is to be hoped that, after Kosovo, it will be much more difficult for the international community to stand aside when tragedies such as the genocide in Rwanda take place. However, the methods were much more in keeping with a traditional conception of war and had little connection with the proclaimed goal. In effect, there were two wars waged simultaneously. First, there was the war waged by Milošević against the Kosovar Albanians. This was an archetypal example of a 'new war' as described in this book and also provided evidence of the way in which this new type of violence tends to spread. Secondly, there was NATO's 'spectacle war' – a type of war whose evolution can be traced through the imaginary war of the Cold War era, the wars in the Falklands and Iraq, as well as the Revolution in Military Affairs to which I refer in the introduction to this book.

These two wars, it can be argued, far from colliding, fed off each other. With hindsight, it can be argued that Milošević may have wanted to be bombed. The Yugoslav army was prepared to withstand attacks of this kind. Bombing provided a cover under which he could carry out an accelerated plan for ethnic cleansing. A week before the bombing began, Serb policemen were marking the houses of Kosovar Albanians with crosses so the 'cleaners' would know where to go. Moreover, once the air strikes began, intensive bombing seems to have been followed by ever-greater acts of brutality.

It may also have been the case that there were those in Western circles, particularly in the USA, who wanted to bomb. The critics of NATO bombing argue that the West could have offered more concessions at the talks in Rambouillet, and later Paris, that preceded the air strikes; the West could have allowed a UN and not a NATO umbrella for a future military presence, for example, and need not have insisted on the far-reaching provisions of the security annex. It is not clear whether this would have made any difference; the main reason for the failure of the talks was Serb intransigence. Nevertheless, there was growing pressure to 'do something' and to 'teach Milošević a lesson'. Once the strikes began, they appeared to be vindicated by Serbian ethnic cleansing. NATO spokesmen triumphantly reported each horrific violation of human rights as though this provided an argument for bombing; they seemed much less able to express remorse, anguish or even frustration at their inability to prevent these terrible events.

In what follows, I shall describe each of these wars in turn. In the last section, I shall discuss what might have been an alternative approach and the implications of different lessons learned from the war over Kosovo for the future of global security.

The 'New War' in Kosovo

The war waged by Milošević in Kosovo was a classic example of a new war. First of all, it was a war waged in the name of the 'new nationalism'. Some might argue that the case for 'ancient hatreds' is much stronger in Kosovo than in Bosnia. The Albanian population is clearly differentiated from the Serbs, both linguistically and ethnically. Moreover, the twentieth century witnessed violence and hostility between the two populations, especially of Serbs and Montenegrins against the Albanians. In the entire post-war period, there has been tension between the two groups: there were very few Albanians in the Communist leadership, and Kosovo was ruled by martial law immediately after the war; from the late 1960s Kosovo increasingly gained self-rule, and the proportion of Albanians grew both because of the higher Albanian birthrate and because of outmigration by Serbs. Under the 1974 constitution, Kosovo was declared an autonomous province within Serbia. In the late 1970s and early 1980s there were pressures from the Albanian population to upgrade Kosovo's status to that of a republic like Croatia or Slovenia.

Nevertheless, as Noel Malcolm shows in his history of Kosovo, the case is by no means clear-cut.[3] For long periods, Albanians and Serbs fought together against the Ottoman and Austrian empires. In the famous Battle of Kosovo, celebrated in Serbian myths, Albanians fought on the same side as the Serbs against the Turks. There were periods of religious cooperation and even syncretism, as well as periods of conflict. Some Albanian and Slav families even claimed common descent.

The current crisis has to be traced to the rise of new nationalism in Yugoslavia, which I have described in chapter 3, and, in particular, to the rise of Slobodan Milošević and the offcial adoption of an extreme Serbian nationalist agenda. The position of the Serb minority in Kosovo and the insistence on the religious importance of Kosovo to the Serbian nation were central elements in the nationalist propaganda developed by Serbian intellectuals and exploited by Milošević. The removal of autonomy from Kosovo by Milošević in 1989 marked the beginning of the disintegration of Yugoslavia. Subsequently, Albanians were dismissed from their jobs in public service and state-owned firms; Albanian students were banned from entering university buildings and a new Serbian curriculum was introduced; and arbitrary arrest and police violence against Albanians became routine practices – Human Rights Watch reported that the record of human rights violations in Kosovo was the worst in Europe.

The growth of nationalist sentiment among Kosovar Albanians in the 1980s and 1990s also had some 'new' elements. Of particular importance was the role of the diaspora, especially in Germany and Switzerland. Many of those who had taken part in protests and student demonstrations in the early 1980s left the country. During the 1990s, a 3 per cent income tax was collected from half a million Kosovar Albanians who lived and worked abroad. Moreover, an Albanian-language television service was run from Switzerland and could be received by those Kosovar Albanians who had satellite dishes. After 1997, when the KLA (the Kosovo Liberation Army) became more influential, the role of the diaspora in switching support was critical.

The Albanian movement also could be said to have reflected some new civic elements. Under the leadership of Ibrahim Rugova, the Kosovar Albanians declared independence and organized their own parallel system of public services, including education, within Kosovo. Influenced by the thinking of the 1989 revolutions, they adopted a non-violent strategy. Indeed, at the height of the tensions in the early 1990s, they decided to abolish the traditional practice of blood feud.[4] According to Rugova, the 'Serbs only wait for a pretext to attack the Albanian population and wipe it out. We believe it is better to do nothing and stay alive than be massacred.'[5]

Secondly, the methods of the war represented a perfection of the techniques developed in Croatia and Bosnia, the strategy of controlling territory through population displacement. Violence was mainly directed against civilians. In the period up to 24 March, when the bombing began, KLA activities were used as an excuse for ethnic cleansing mainly by regular Yugoslav forces and Serb police – some 400,000 people left the country before the bombing began. Once it started, the pattern of ethnic cleansing was systematic and organized. Ethnic cleansing was carried out by a combination of regular forces and paramilitary groups augmented by criminals released from prison for the purpose. Local Serbs were also mobilized. Just as in Bosnia, the role of the regular forces was to shell a particular area; then, when the local people were sufficiently weakened and terrorized, the paramilitary groups would enter the area, separating men from women and children, looting all valuables, including documents, burning homes and destroying historic and cultural symbols. Refugees report that 'cleansers' had informed them that they were under instructions to 'clean' Kosovo within a week. The logistical arrangements for trains and buses to deport Kosovar Albanians clearly illustrate the planned character of the ethnic cleansing.

One of the most notorious paramilitary groups in Kosovo was known as 'Frenki's boys'. According to intelligence sources, Franko Simatović was the link between Milošević and freelance paramilitary groups. Reportedly, Frenki's Boys had their headquarters at the back of a dress shop in Djakovica. They wore cowboy hats over ski masks, and painted Indian stripes on their faces. Their trademark was the sign of the Serbian Chetniks and a silhouette of a destroyed city with the words 'City Breakers' in English.[6]

The evidence now available suggests that some 10,000 people were killed in the cleansing operation, including children, and that more than a million were forced to leave the country. When NATO forces entered in June, only 600,000 people were left in Kosovo and, of these, 400,000 were internally displaced.[7]

On the Albanian side, the KLA represented a mixture of paramilitary-type forces and self-defence forces. The KLA grew out of a party formed in the diaspora in the early 1980s called the LPK (Levizja Popullare e Kosoves). It claimed to be a Leninist organization, drawing its inspiration from the Albanian leader Enver Hoxha. In the early 1990s it set up a guerrilla group, which, at that time, had little support within Kosovo.

Several factors changed the position of the KLA. One was the growing frustration with Rugova's non-violent methods after Dayton. As Veton Surroi, one of the most significant independent intellectuals, put it, Dayton demonstrated that 'ethnic territories have legitimacy' and that 'international attention can only be obtained through war'.[8] This was a period when efforts to sustain parallel institutions were becoming exhausted and many young people, denied an official education, were disenchanted with what they saw as the passive approach of Ibrahim Rugova. A second factor was the sudden availability of arms after the Albanian state collapsed in the summer of 1997; arms caches were opened and hundreds of thousands of Kalashnikovs were available for sale at a few dollars each. And a third factor was the fact that many Kosovar Albanians abroad switched their donations to the 'Homeland Calling' fund organized by the KLA.

Nevertheless, it was not until 1998 that the KLA became a significant political force within Kosovo. On 28 February 1998, the Serbs decided to arrest a local brigand in Prekaz called Adem Jashari, who was associated with the KLA; within a week, 80 members of his extended family were dead. Subsequently, local militias calling themselves the KLA were formed all over Kosovo to defend villages. The rapid growth of the KLA provided the excuse for the activities of Serb forces in the summer and autumn of 1998. As became clear, however, the KLA was no match for Serb forces – at least, not until the very end of the NATO bombing campaign. There were no battles. Under attack from the Serbs, the KLA melted into the hills and woods.

Finally, the Kosovo conflict also displayed a characteristic new war economy. Kosovo was always one of the poorest regions of Yugoslavia. After the removal of autonomy, the formal economy declined rapidly. Unemployment was extremely high and there was a large grey economy, estimated at 70 per cent of the total economy.[9] On the Serb side, the paramilitary groups and criminals appear to have been paid for their work. Payslips were found showing that Frenki's Boys received 130DM a month. Young men in Republika Serbska were offered a similar amount to go and fight in Kosovo. Loot and pillage were also a reward for atrocities. In addition, families were forced to part with all their savings in order to be allowed to leave and not be killed. On the Albanian side, the KLA was dependent largely on the Albanian diaspora. They do seem to have had connections with Kosovars involved in the drug trade in Zurich who helped with money and arms.

The eruption of violence in Kosovo has to be understood in terms of the tendency of this kind of violence to spread. Clearly there were growing tensions within Kosovo. But the societal ripples from the wars in Croatia and Bosnia should not be underestimated. Just when the international community was congratulating itself for containing the conflict in Bosnia, the violence was spreading through the political effects of Dayton, through the impact of the criminalized economy on neighbouring states, particularly Albania, and through the unsavoury networks established by Milošević, which developed a vested interest in continuing violence both to retain power positions and to find new sources of income.

NATO's 'Spectacle War'

Throughout the spring of 1998, Western leaders were making strong statements about their determination to prevent war in Kosovo. 'We are not going to stand by and watch the Serb authorities do in Kosovo what they can no longer get away with in Bosnia', said Madeleine Albright in March. Similar pronouncements were made by the UN Secretary General, NATO's Secretary General and by various foreign and defence ministers.

However, the method chosen to prevent war was diplomacy backed by the threat of air strikes. I argued in chapter 3 that a weak form of humanitarian intervention was introduced in Bosnia and that the most important lesson of the Bosnian war was the need to strengthen this type of intervention – the establishment of safe havens and humanitarian corridors need to be backed by robust peacekeeping on the ground. This was not the conclusion drawn by Western leaders. They believed that the Dayton Agreement was the consequence of diplomacy backed by force and that what was needed was another Dayton-type agreement for Kosovo. They did not take into account the fact that the Dayton Agreement was finally reached after four years of war and after ethnic cleansing was almost complete; unlike the situation in Kosovo, the parties had reached a point where they needed an agreement, and they needed the international community to legitimize an agreement.

Despite their brave words, it was not until October, amidst public concern about a looming humanitarian crisis, that Richard Holbrooke, the architect of Dayton, negotiated a preliminary deal with Milošević. The negotiations were backed by the threat of air strikes. The agreement reached was very weak. It placed limits on Serb forces, and it introduced OSCE 'verifiers' into the region. Holbrooke now says that he was not able to negotiate a stronger agreement because of the American refusal to contemplate ground troops: 'I was not able to negotiate armed international security forces in Kosovo in October because it was not possible to do that under the instructions I was given.'[10]

The agreement, however, did not last. Although, initially, violence subsided, the monitors failed to prevent the KLA from moving into the areas vacated by the withdrawal of Serb forces. By early 1999, the Serbs began to introduce new forces into the region. Indeed, there was mounting evidence of a planned offensive. The massacre of 40 people at Račak triggered off a new round of diplomacy, culminating in the Rambouillet Agreement which envisaged a three-year transitional period of autonomy for Kosovo, although the Serbs would have retained control of certain key functions, and a substantial NATO presence on the ground. Under pressure from the Americans, the Albanians signed the agreement.

When the Serbs refused to sign the agreement, a bombing campaign was inevitable. Some Western leaders claim that they were taken by surprise by the accelerated ethnic cleansing. But it was quite clear that this was likely to happen. It was reported that Western intelligence knew about a plan called Operation Horseshoe as far back as September, although this has never been substantiated. Reportedly, the Yugoslav General Sreten Lukić told members of the Kosovo verification mission: 'Give us a week and we will clean the terrorists out of Kosovo.' Likewise, Seselj, the leader of the Serbian Radical Party and Deputy Prime Minister of Serbia, warned on television, one week before the bombing began, that 'not a single Albanian would remain if NATO bombed'.

The air strikes went ahead perhaps because of miscalculations about the reaction of Milošević; it was hoped he would agree within a few days. But, more importantly, they went ahead because Western leaders felt that it would look worse if they did nothing, and since the Americans, at least, were unwilling to commit ground troops, bombing, which had the advantage of offering an impressive television spectacle, was the only option on the table. The risks of inaction were made clear by Xavier Solana, then NATO Secretary General, in an article in the *International Herald Tribune* a week after the bombing began.

The preference for bombing as a military strategy has to be understood in terms of a combination of American domestic politics and institutional interests. Every US government since the Second World War has built a domestic consensus around the idea of defending America from external enemies making use of superior technology. The imaginary war of the Cold War period and the casualty-free televised wars from the air of recent times serve to keep alive the idea of external enemies, while minimizing the risk of unpopularity as a result of the horrors of real war. The idea of 'rogue states' that might sponsor terrorists armed with mass destruction, as promoted by Madeleine Albright, is the latest substitute for the Soviet threat of earlier times; both Serbia and Iraq are the prime candidates for this role. The threat from 'rogue states' is supposed to justify renewed expenditure on air power.

This political concern is underpinned by the institutional interests of the defence industry, the technological enthusiasts and the air force, which has led to the evolution of expensive and sophisticated long-distance weapons making use of new developments in information technology. The latest phase in this evolution is known as the Revolution in Military Affairs (RMA) and its paradigmatic expression is the Tomahawk cruise missile. The RMA offers politicians the possibility of 'intervention anywhere, any place, with minimum casualties'.[11]

In practice, however, the utility of the air strikes was highly questionable. Altogether, some 36,000 sorties were flown, of which 12,000 were strike sorties. Some 20,000 'smart' bombs and 5,000 conventional bombs were dropped. But it appears that not much damage was done to the Yugoslav military machine. For fifty years, the Yugoslav army had been trained to withstand a superior enemy. A vast underground network had been built, including stores, airports and barracks. Tactics had been developed which involved constructing decoys, hiding tanks and artillery, conserving air defences and avoiding troop concentrations. NATO did not succeed, in the initial stages, in knocking out the Yugoslav air-defence system: this is why NATO aircraft continued to fly at 15,000 feet. Nor did they succeed in doing much damage to Serb forces on the ground. NATO claims that the air strikes did constrain Serb forces and prevented them from bringing equipment into the open, but, nevertheless, the air strikes evidently did not prevent operations against Kosovar Albanian civilians. In particular, NATO appears to have had a poor record in hitting armour. Despite higher claims, only 26 'tank carcasses' were found in Kosovo after the Serbs withdrew.[12] Moreover, some 40,000 Yugoslav troops left Kosovo, suggesting that rather few had been lost.

There was more success in hitting civilian targets – roads, bridges, power stations, oil depots and factories. Because of the insistence that aircraft fly above 15,000 feet, pilots could not see what was happening on the ground and were dependent on intelligence from numerous, often badly coordinated, sources. Consequently, repeated mistakes were made, as became embarrassingly clear for the duration of the air strikes. Low points included the bombing of the Chinese Embassy and the bombing of refugees inside Kosovo. Some 1,400 people were killed in so-called 'collateral damage'. Environmentalists are only now assessing the consequences of damage to industrial facilities. Historic sites were destroyed, in Novi Sad for example. A TV transmitter was destroyed, killing journalists inside. And targets were hit in Montenegro, whose government had refused to participate in the war in Kosovo.

The political consequences of this type of bombing were counterproductive. Despite the insistence of NATO spokesmen that there is a big difference between killing by mistake and killing deliberately, this difference was not obvious to the victims of the bombing. Who determines whether the killing of civilians counts as a 'massacre' or as 'collateral damage'? Likewise, the insistence of Western leaders that the bombing was directed against the regime and not against Serbs was not at all evident to those who experienced its effects.

The air strikes mobilized Serbian national sentiment, allowing Milošević to crack down on NGOs and independent media during the war and thus minimize domestic constraints against his activities in Kosovo. Together with the influx of refugees, the air strikes polarized opinion in both Macedonia and Montenegro, accentuating domestic tensions and the risk of the further spread of violence. They also polarized international opinion: for many in the East, the claim that this was a war for human rights was viewed as a cover for the pursuit of Western imperial interests in the Balkans.

In the end, Milošević capitulated and agreed to NATO's demands. Could it be argued that this was a victory for the air strategy? Right up until the last few days, no one expected that he would capitulate. Crucial factors seem to have been the destruction of civilian infrastructure, the loss of support from some of Milošević's inner circle and, above all, the intervention of the Russians, who made it clear that they could not continue to support the Yugoslav position. It is also sometimes claimed that Milošević was influenced by NATO discussions about ground intervention, although even if, as is claimed, a decision were imminent, it would have taken some time to organize.

The capitulation of Milošević allowed the refugees to return to Kosovo. But the trauma of ethnic cleansing can never be reversed. The failure to prevent ethnic cleansing and the vacuum created after the withdrawal of the Serbs has greatly strengthened the position of the KLA. Some 160,000 Serb refugees have left Kosovo since NATO entered the province. Instead of preserving multicultural values, NATO is protecting an ethnically homogenous Albanian enclave.

Some argue that the air strikes contributed to the fall of Milošević in October 2000. Undoubtedly, together with economic sanctions, they helped to precipitate economic collapse, but they also helped to entrench embittered anti-Western nationalistic attitudes that persist even after Milošević.

An Alternative Approach

'Spectacle wars', like 'new wars', presuppose exclusivist categories of human beings. Western lives are privileged over other lives. In order to prevent NATO casualties, the lives of civilians were risked, including the lives of those whom the operation was designed to protect.

A cosmopolitan approach to the Kosovo crisis would have been aimed directly at protecting people. There should have been a humanitarian intervention on the ground aimed at minimizing all casualties, even if this meant risking the lives of international troops. Humanitarian intervention is different from air strikes and different from classic 'old war' ground operations; the goal is the prevention of gross violations of human rights, not the defeat of an enemy. Humanitarian intervention is defensive and non-escalatory by definition. Its focus is the individual human being and not another state. Humanitarian intervention also has to involve respect for the rule of law and support for democracy. Effectively, it constitutes cosmopolitan law-enforcement and is thus more like policing than war fighting.

The kind of intervention that was undertaken in Bosnia – the establishment of safe havens and humanitarian corridors – represents a model, albeit weak, for this kind of operation. Such an intervention would require close air support but not a wider destructive air campaign. It would also require heavy equipment and firepower, which would be used very selectively. Some European armed forces, notably those of Britain and Denmark, have made use of the lessons of Bosnia to retrain their forces for this type of operation.

If possible such an intervention should be based on consent. But instead of high-level negotiations aimed at finding a political compromise between irreconcilable parties, negotiations should have focused on the position on the ground. The goal was to establish an international presence in Kosovo, not to resolve the issue of status. Instead of backing negotiations with the threat of air strikes, the negotiations should have been backed up by the NATO position on the ground in neighbouring Macedonia.

Humanitarian intervention, by protecting people and enforcing law, can create the conditions for a cosmopolitan political response. The aim is to establish a secure environment where people can act freely without fear and where inclusive forms of politics can be nurtured. Ways have to be found to sideline those responsible for ethnic cleansing, not to elevate them through negotiations. The indictment of Milošević and some of his co-conspirators the week before the bombing ended was a constructive step in this direction. Targeted sanctions such as the denial of visas or the freezing of bank accounts could also be applied. An intervention of this kind would have made it more difficult for Milošević to justify his behaviour within Yugoslavia and it would have generated much more international support.

What happens in the future depends on what lessons are learned from the wars over Kosovo. There is a tendency for politicians to believe their own 'spin'. The success of air strikes in terms of domestic public opinion may be all that matters to them. If this is the case, then we can expect increased investment in air power and more 'spectacle wars'. We can anticipate a world in which 'new wars' justify 'spectacle wars', and vice versa. Indeed, the distinction between 'new wars' and 'spectacle wars' may begin to blur. We can expect a further spread of 'new wars' and, from time to time, a 'spectacle war' to reassure the public that politicians care about violations of human rights in other parts of the world and are ready to act.

The alternative lesson is that NATO partially redeemed itself after a catastrophic defeat in the first week when the very development it was supposed to prevent – namely the ethnic cleansing of Kosovo – took place. Given the unwillingness of the Americans to commit ground troops, Europeans should be better prepared to carry the main burden of this type of operation in the future. Moreover, the readiness to undertake humanitarian intervention has to be part of a broader overall strategy to support democrats and to stimulate productive economic development so as to provide an alternative to the network of extremist politics and criminality.

The Stability Pact for the Balkans and the proposal for a 'Marshall Plan' are welcome steps in this direction, all the more so since the fall of Milošević. It is especially important to foster all kinds of people-to-people exchanges so as to strengthen and empower 'islands of civility' in the region and to open up Serbia to dialogue and cooperation.

Which lesson is correct is likely to be a continuing debate. The first lesson will be learned by realists, by those who favour futures outlined by the likes of Samuel Huntington or Robert Kaplan. The second lesson will be favoured by the cosmopolitans and those who still believe it is possible to build a set of global arrangements that can incorporate the democratic control of violence.

Notes

Chapter 1   Introduction

1 The research project was undertaken for the United Nations University's World Institute for Development Economics Research (UNU/WIDER). The results are published in Mary Kaldor and Basker Vashee (eds), *Restructuring the Global Military Sector: Volume I: New Wars* (Cassell/Pinter, London, 1997).

2 David Keen, 'When war itself is privatized', *Times Literary Supplement*, December 1995.

3 Mark Duffield, 'Post-modern conflict: warlords, post-adjustment states and private protection', *Journal of Civil Wars*, April 1998; Michael Ignatieff, *The Warrior's Honor: Ethnic War and the Modern Conscience* (Chatto and Windus, London, 1998).

4 Chris Hables Gray, *Post-Modern War: The New Politics of Conflicts* (Routledge, London and New York, 1997).

5 Martin Shaw, 'War and globality: the role and character of war in the global transition', in Ho-Won Jeong (ed.), *Peace and Conflict: A New Agenda* (Dartmouth Publishing, forthcoming).

6 See David Jablonsky, *The Owl of Minerva Flies at Night: Doctrinal Change and Continuity and the Revolution in Military Affairs* (US Army War College, Carlisle Barracks, PA,1994); Elliott Cohen, 'A revolution in warfare', *Foreign Affairs* (March/April 1996); Robert J. Bunker, 'Technology in a neo-Clausewitzean setting', in Gert de Nooy (ed.), *The Clausewitzean Dictum and the Future of Western Military Strategy* (Netherlands Institute of International Relations, 'Clingendael', Kluwer Law International, 1997).

7 Jean Baudrillard, *The Gulf War* (Power Publishers, London, 1995).

8 See Malcolm Waters, *Globalization* (Routledge, London, 1995); David Held, *Democracy and the Global Order: From the Modern State to Cosmopolitan Governance* (Polity Press, Cambridge, 1995).

9 See Mary Kaldor, Ulrich Albrecht and Asbjörn Eide, *The International Military Order* (Macmillan, London, 1978).

10 Anthony Giddens makes a similar argument about the new political cleavage between cosmopolitanism and fundamentalism. See Anthony Giddens, *Beyond Left and Right: The Future of Radical Politics* (Stanford University Press, Stanford, CA, 1994).

11 On the concept of the mode of warfare, see Mary Kaldor, 'Warfare and capitalism', in E. P. Thompson *et al.*, *Exterminism and Cold War* (Verso, London, 1981).

12 In addition to the research project undertaken for UNU / WIDER, I and my colleagues at the Sussex European Institute undertook a research project in 1995 on Balkan reconstruction for the European Commission. See Vesna Bojičić, Mary Kaldor and Ivan Vejvoda, 'Post-war reconstruction in the Balkans', *SEI Working Paper* (Sussex European Institute, 1995). A shorter updated version is published in *European Foreign Affairs Review*, 2, 3 (Autumn 1997).

Chapter 2   Old Wars

1 According to Clausewitz: 'War belongs not to the province of Arts and Sciences but to the province of social life . . . It would be better instead of comparing it with any Art, to liken it to business competition, which is also a conflict of human interests and activities.' *On War* (first published 1832) (Pelican Books, London, 1968), p. 202.

2 Clausewitz, *On War*, p. 1.

3 Martin van Creveld, *The Transformation of War* (Free Press, Macmillan, London, 1991).

4 John Keegan, *A History of Warfare* (Hutchinson, London, 1993), p. 12.

5 Michael Roberts, 'The military revolution 1560–1660', in David B. Ralston, *Soldiers and States: Civil–Military Relations in Modern Europe* (Heath and Company, Boston, 1966), p. 18.

6 Max Weber, *The Theory of Social and Economic Organization*, translated and edited by A. M. Henderson and Talcott Parsons (Free Press, Macmillan, London, 1947), p. 326.

7 Van Creveld, *Transformation of War*, p. 41.

8 I am indebted to Robert Neild for some of these points. See 'The Evolution of Clean Government', Trinity College, Cambridge, unpublished MS, 1997.

9 See Charles Tilly, *Coercion, Capital and European States* AD *990–*

1990 (Blackwell, Oxford, 1990); Michael Mann, *States, War and Capitalism* (Blackwell, Oxford, 1988).

[10] Anthony Giddens, *The Nation-State and Violence* (Polity Press, Cambridge, 1985).

[11] Theda Skocpol, *States and Social Revolutions* (Cambridge University Press, Cambridge, 1979).

[12] 'Abstract and judgment of Saint-Pierre's project for perpetual peace' (1756), in Stanley Hoffman and David P. Fidler, *Rousseau on International Relations* (Oxford University Press, Oxford, 1991), pp. 90–1.

[13] 'Perpetual peace' (1795), in Hans Reiss (ed.), *Kant's Political Writings* (Cambridge University Press, Cambridge, 1992).

[14] Clausewitz, *On War*, p. 12.

[15] See Richard Simkin, *Race to the Swift: Thoughts on Twenty First Century Warfare* (Brasseys Defence Publishers, London, 1985).

[16] Clausewitz, *On War*, p. 102.

[17] The St Petersburg Declaration of 1868, which limited weapons that cause unnecessary suffering, read as follows:

> Considering that the progress of civilization should have the effect of alleviating as much as possible the calamities of war;
>   That the only legitimate object which states should endeavour to accomplish during war is to weaken the military forces of society;
>   That for this purpose it is sufficient to disable the greatest possible number of men;
>   That this object would be exceeded by the employment of arms which uselessly aggravate the sufferings of disabled men or render their death inevitable;
>   That the employment of such arms would therefore be contrary to the laws of humanity.

Quoted in Michael Howard, 'Constraints on warfare', in Michael Howard, George J. Andreopoulos and Mark R. Shulman (eds), *Constraints on Warfare in the Western World: The Laws of War* (Yale University Press, New Haven and London, 1994).

[18] This crime against humanity, as it was labelled after the war, did not technically count as a violation of the nineteenth-century laws of war, as Adam Roberts points out, since it took place in occupied territory. See Adam Roberts, 'Land warfare: from Hague to Nuremberg', in Howard, Andreopoulos and Shulman, *Constraints on Warfare*.

[19] See Ernest Gellner, *The Conditions of Liberty: Civil Society and its Rivals* (Hamish Hamilton, London, 1994).

[20] Edward N. Luttwak, 'Towards post-heroic warfare', *Foreign Affairs*, 74, 3 (May/June 1995).

[21] Gabriel Kolko, *A Century of War: Politics, Conflicts, and Society since 1914* (New Press, New York, 1994).

[22] This is explored in my book *The Baroque Arsenal* (Andre Deutsch, London, 1982).

[23] See, for example, Lawrence Freedman, *The Evolution of Nuclear Strategy* (Macmillan, London, 1981).

[24] The issue has been extensively discussed in the pages of the American journal *International Security*. Key studies include Michael Doyle 'Liberalism and world politics' *American Political Science Review*, 80, 4 (December 1986); Bruce Russett, *Grasping the Democratic Peace: Principles for a Post-Cold War World* (Princeton University Press, Princeton, 1993).

[25] Claus Offe, 'Western nationalism, Eastern nationalism, and the problems of post-communist transition', *Europe and the Balkans International Network* (Bologna, 1996).

[26] Van Creveld, *Transformation of War*, p. 16.

Chapter 3   Bosnia–Herzgovina: A Case Study of a New War

[1] The war may not yet have ended. At the time of writing, the Dayton Agreement is being implemented. This could turn out to be merely an interlude in the fighting.

[2] He said: 'I understand your frustration but you have a situation that is better than ten other places in the world . . . I can give you a list.' Quoted in David Rieff, *Slaughter House: Bosnia and the Failure of the West* (New York, Vintage, 1995), p. 24.

[3] *Final Report of the Commission of Experts Pursuant to Security Council Resolution 780 (1992)*, S/1994/674, 27 May 1994, vol. I, annex IV, par. 84.

[4] The story is contained in a collection of Ivo Andrić's short stories published in *The Damned Yard and Other Stories* (Forest Books, London and Boston, 1992.) At the end of the story, the young man volunteers to fight in the Spanish Civil War, where he is killed in an air raid. 'Thus ended the life of a man who ran away from hatred', says Andric. Does this mean that hatred is everywhere? Or that, in volunteering to fight in Spain, he had some hopes of overcoming hatred?

[5] Perhaps this was because the perception corresponded to the world view of European politicians themselves. David Owen's book is peppered with remarks that suggest that he himself categorizes people in national terms. Thus, for example, Ćosić, the then Yugoslav President, is described as showing 'some of the qualities that have made and will in future make Serbs a substantial people'. The challenge for the negotiations is to devise a structure which preserves the integrity of Bosnia–Herzegovina but allows the Serbs to 'preserve and safeguard their national identity'. See David Owen, *A Balkan*

Odyssey (Victor Gollancz, London,1995), pp. 48, 67.

⁶ 'Croats belong to a different culture – a different civilisation from the Serbs. Croats are part of Western Europe, part of the Mediterranean tradition. Long before Shakespeare and Molière, our writers were translated into European languages. The Serbs belong to the East. They are Eastern people, like the Turks and Albanians. They belong to the Byzantine culture . . . Despite similarities in language, we cannot be together.' Quoted in Leonard J. Cohen, *Broken Bonds: Yugoslavia's Disintegration and Balkan Politics in Transition* (Westview Press, Oxford and Boulder, CO, 1995), p. 211.

⁷ See for example, A. D. Smith, *Theories of Nationalism* (Duckworth, London, 1971).

⁸ According to Sead Fetahagic, a member of Circle 99, the association of independent intellectuals in Sarajevo: 'Many of us are opposed to this multiculturalism because multiculturalism has accepted the manner in which the West has accepted it – one culture alongside another culture alongside a third culture. But we in Bosnia–Herzegovina have always had one culture. I have been brought up within the Serb, Croat, Muslim, Jewish, Czech, European and American culture. We think that one culture exists and not several which are developed one next to the other.' 'The Force of Irreality', *hCa Quarterly*, 15, 16 (Winter/Spring, 1996). Likewise, according to a sociological study undertaken in 1939, 'a feeling of real ethnic and characterlogical unity remains alive alongside all the historical and national-political differentiation', quoted in Cohen, *Broken Bonds*, pp. 19–20.

⁹ See Ernest Gellner, *Nations and Nationalism* (Basil Blackwell, Oxford, 1983).

¹⁰ See Ivan Vejvoda 'Yugoslavia 1945–91 – from decentralisation without democracy to dissolution', in D. A. Dyker and I. Vejvoda, *Yugoslavia and After: A Study in Fragmentation, Despair and Rebirth* (Longmans, London and New York, 1996).

¹¹ For a more extensive discussion of this, see Susan Woodward, *Socialist Unemployment: The Political Economy of Yugoslavia 1945–90* (Princeton University Press, Princeton, 1995); Vesna Bojičić and Mary Kaldor, 'The political economy of the war in Bosnia–Herzegovina', in Mary Kaldor and Basker Vashee (eds), *Restructuring the Global Military Sector: Volume I: New Wars* (Cassell / Pinter, London, 1997).

¹² See David Dyker, 'The degeneration of the Yugoslav Communist Party as a managing elite – a familiar East European story?', in Dyker and Vejvoda, *Yugoslavia and After*.

¹³ See Mark Thompson, *Forging War: The Media in Serbia, Croatia, and Bosnia–Herzegovina* (Article XIX, London, 1994).

14 See James Gow, *Legitimacy and the Military: The Yugoslav Crisis* (Pinter, London, 1992).

15 See Milos Vasić, 'The Yugoslav Army and the post-Yugoslav armies', in Dyker and Vejvoda, *Yugoslavia and After*.

16 Rieff, *Slaughter House*, p. 103.

17 'To invite the emigration back to the homeland for a great meeting was risky to the point that even those people who were later in my leadership waited till the last minute to see whether we would be arrested or not. This is why that was a turning point in my life in terms of decision-making . . . Great deeds, both in individual creative terms, and especially in social innovation, and even militarily, are created on the razor's edge between the possible and the impossible.' Quoted in Laura Silber and Alan Little, *The Death of Yugoslavia* (Penguin Books, London, 1995), p. 91.

18 Xavier Bougarel, 'Etat et Communautarisme en Bosnie–Herzegovina', unpublished MS; English version in Dyker and Vejvoda, *Yugoslavia and After*.

19 Private interview with the author.

20 For example, one of its editorials wrote: 'Instinctively every Muslim would wish to save his Serb neighbour instead of the reverse, however, every Muslim must name a Serb and take an oath to kill him.' 1 April 1993, quoted in Mazowiecki Report E/CN.4/1994/3, 5 May 1993.

21 I am indebted to my doctoral student Neven Andjelić for detailed information about the pre-war peace movement. The story of Bosnian civil society is told in his Master's thesis, 'The Rise and Fall of Civil Society in Bosnia–Herzegovina', Sussex: Sussex University, 1995.

22 According to one of his fellow students: 'Many people will tell you now that they saw the war coming then, but I didn't and I don't think Suada (the student who died) did either . . . As a medical student scheduled to graduate in May, Suada could easily have stayed away from the demonstration that day. She wasn't from Sarajevo. She wasn't even Bosnian . . . It was not an angry crowd . . . The people around us, most of them young, were good-humoured and eager to make their point in a peaceful way. I was about fifty metres from the bridge when a few shots – maybe five or six – rang out. Everybody began to run. Once we got to cover behind a building, I was incredibly angry. It had never occurred to me that someone would open fire on a group of unarmed demonstrators. Strange to say, war still didn't seem inevitable. It was only a few days later that there seemed no turning back, that we began to speak of Suada as the first person killed in the Bosnian war. What had seemed a random act of violence, a great personal tragedy, slowly took shape in

our minds as the first incident in a far greater drama: Europe's worst war in fifty years.' Quoted in Silber and Little, *The Death of Yugoslavia*, pp. 251–2.

[23] 'Dans un ultime sursault, la société civile bosniaque naissante a tenté d'évincer le communautarisme de la sphère politique. Un moment destabilisées, les parties nationalistes se vengent en faisant entrer la guerre dans la vie quotidienne.' Bougarel, 'Etat et Communautarisme'.

[24] *Report on the Situation of Human Rights in the Territory of Former Yugoslavia*, United Nations, E/CN.4/1992/S–1/9, New York, 28 August 1992, par. 17.

[25] Stockholm International Peace Research Institute, *SIPRI Yearbook 1992: World Armaments and Disarmament* (OUP, Oxford, 1992).

[26] Ibid.

[27] The same company has been used since the Dayton Agreement to train the army of the Federation of Bosnia–Herzegovina. See David Shearer, 'Private Armies and Military Intervention', *Adelphi Paper 316* (IISS, London, February 1998).

[28] *Final Report of the Commission of Experts.*

[29] This was a point generally missed by those who advocated lifting the arms embargo on Bosnia–Herzegovina as a solution to the war. Whatever symbolic significance this may have had, it would have had little practical significance, since whether or not the Bosnian army received arms depended on the attitude of the Croatian government. Perhaps the most positive consequence would have been the circumventing of illegal arms dealers in Zagreb.

[30] Reports in both the Croatian and Serbian press refer to cooperation between the JNA and Croat factories to produce M-84 tanks. There were also reports that all three sides in Bosnia–Herzegovina co-operated in the production of ammunition because even the 7.62 mm rifle bullet contained components that were produced by the different sides. See Milan Nikolić, 'The Burden of the Military Heritage', unpublished paper produced for WIDER, Helsinki, 1993.

[31] *Final Report of the Commission of Experts*, Annex IV, 'Ethnic Cleansing', par. 238.

[32] His doctoral thesis, which he completed in 1976, was on Marxist justifications for war.

[33] *Final Report of the Commission of Experts*, Annex IV, 'Ethnic Cleansing', par. 103.

[34] Ibid., Annex III A, 'Special Forces', par. 68.

[35] See Vasić, 'The Yugoslav Army', p. 129.

[36] Silber and Little, *The Death of Yugoslavia*, p. 270.

[37] Shems Hadj-Nassar, 'Has Rape been Used as a Systematic Weapon of War in the Conflict in the Former Yugoslavia?' University of

Sussex, unpublished Master's thesis, 1995.

38 Ethnic cleansing continued in Banja Luka and in Bijeljina and Janja right up to the end of the war. UNHCR reported one man arriving in Tuzla at the end of 1994: 'There are no more children, no more friends, no more information, no more life, no more Mosques and no more graveyards.' UNHCR, *Information Notes on Former Yugoslavia*, 11/1994, Zagreb, November 1994.

39 Mazowiecki Report E/CN.4/1994/3, 5 May 1993.

40 *Final Report of the Commission of Experts*, Annex III A, 'Special Forces', par. 70.

41 At Dretelj, 'Victims stated that they were subjected to sexual torture, beaten with truncheons and sticks, burned with cigarettes and candles, and forced to drink urine and eat grass. One victim reported that she was held in a room with three other professional women for ten days during which time women in the room were raped repeatedly.' Ibid., par. 67.

42 Vasić, 'The Yugoslav Army', p. 134.

43 *Final Report of the Commission of Experts*, Annex III, par. 239. Interestingly, during the war in Croatia, an internal JNA memo stated that Arkan and Šešelj were dangerous to 'military morale' and that their 'primary motive was not fighting against the enemy but robbery of private property and inhuman treatment of Croatian citizens', ibid., par. 100.

44 Xavier Bougarel, *L'Anatomie d'un conflit* (Edition Découverts, Paris, 1995).

45 *Final Report of the Commission of Experts*, Annex III, par. 102.

46 Ibid., Annex IV, par. 142.

47 Alex de Waal, 'Contemporary Warfare in Africa', in Kaldor and Vashee (eds), *Restructuring the Global Military Sector*.

48 This was a German initiative supported only reluctantly by the other European countries. In fact, under German pressure, the EU appointed the Badinter Commission to report on the criteria for recognition for all Yugoslav successor states. In the event, only Macedonia and Slovenia met the criteria for satisfactory arrangements for minorities, but Macedonia's recognition was delayed because of Greek objections.

49 Owen himself suggests that a settlement could have been reached much earlier had the international community been more united and had the negotiators had the full backing of the Americans. He blames the lack of American support for the failure to impose the Vance–Owen Plan in the summer of 1993. It is certainly true that when the Americans took charge, much more was achieved, as in the case of the Washington Agreement and the Dayton Agreement. But this argument misses the politics of the period; there was great

reluctance to impose partition. A different proposal, say a protectorate, might have mobilized international support. By the time the Dayton Agreement was reached, most people had given up on the alternatives to partition.

50 See Pierre Hassner, 'Ex-Yougoslavie: Le Tournant?', *Politique International*, Autumn 1995.

51 As Carrington recalls: 'When I talked to Presidents Tudjman and Milošević, it was quite clear to me that both of them had a solution which was mutually satisfactory, which was that they were going to carve it up between them. They were going to carve Bosnia up. The Serb (areas) would go to Serbia and the Croat (areas) to Croatia. And they weren't worried too much, either of them, about what was going to happen to the Muslims.' Quoted in Silber and Little, *The Death of Yugoslavia*, p. 210.

52 Owen insists that he did treat Izetbegović differently because he was the President, but this was not the public impression and that, after all, was what mattered.

53 UN Department of Public Information, *United Nations Peace-Keeping Information Notes: Update December 1994*, DPI/1306/Rev.4, New York, March 1995, p. 104.

54 SCR 836 extended the mandate of UNPROFOR to protect the safe areas 'to deter attacks against the safe areas . . . to promote the withdrawal of military and para-military units other than those of the Government of the Republic of Bosnia and Herzegovina and to occupy some key points on the ground.' It authorized UNPROFOR 'acting in self-defence, to take all the necessary measures, including the use of force, in reply to bombardments against the safe areas by any of the parties or to armed incursion into them or in the event of any deliberate obstruction in or around those areas to the freedom of movement of UNPROFOR or of protected humanitarian convoys.' And it decided that 'Member States, acting nationally or through regional organisations or arrangements [i.e. NATO] may take, under the authority of the Security Council and subject to close co-ordination with the Secretary-General and UNPROFOR, all necessary measures through the use of air power, in and around the safe areas in Bosnia and Herzegovina to support UNPROFOR.' UN Department of Public Information, *The United Nations and Former Yugoslavia*, DPI/1312/Rev.2, New York, 15 March 1994, p. 136.

55 This was a proposal put forward at the beginning of the war by the Bosnian peace movement. It was discussed as a proposal for negotiation; the idea was that Izetbegović would have been satisfied by preserving the integrity of Bosnia and Herzegovina and that the Serbs would have been satisfied by the removal of the SDA from power.

It was considered seriously in the autumn of 1992 but rejected on the ground that it would have been too costly in both military and financial terms.

[56] Mazowiecki 6th Report, E/CN 4/1994/110, 21 February 1994, par. 347.
[57] Quoted in Rieff, *Slaughter House*, p. 211.
[58] Owen, *A Balkan Odyssey*, p. 354. This was not the case for men on the ground whom I talked to.
[59] Allied Forces Southern Europe, Public Information, *Fact Sheet: Operation Deliberate Force*, Naples, 6 November 1995.
[60] Zdravko Grebo, 'An appeal for realistic expectations', in *hCa Quarterly*, 15, 16 (Winter/Spring, 1996).

Chapter 4   The Politics of New Wars

[1] Ernest Gellner, *Nations and Nationalism* (Blackwell, Oxford, 1983).
[2] Paul Hirst and Grahame Thompson, *Globalization in Question: The International Economy and the Possibilities of Governance* (Polity Press, Cambridge, 1996).
[3] C. Freeman, J. Clarke and L. Soete, *Unemployment and Technical Innovation: A Study of Long Waves and Economic Development* (Frances Pinter, London, 1982); C. Perez-Perez, 'Micro-electronics, long waves, and world structural change', *World Development*, 13, 3 (1985).
[4] See Margit Mayer, 'The shifting local political system in European cities', in Mick Dunford and Grigoris Kafkalas, *The Global–Local Interplay and Spatial Development Strategies* (Belhaven Press, London, 1992); also Manuel Castells and Peter Hall, *Technopoles of the World: The Making of 21st Century Industrial Complexes* (Routledge, London, 1994).
[5] Figures on the upsurge of private, non-profit activities in various parts of the world, sometimes known as the 'associational' revolution, are provided in Lester M. Salamon, 'The rise of the non-profit sector', *Foreign Affairs*, July/August 1994.
[6] Nikolai Bukharin, *Economics of the Transformation Period* (Bergman, New York, 1971).
[7] Robert Reich, *The Work of Nations: Preparing Ourselves for 21st Century Capitalism* (Simon and Schuster, London, 1993), p. 97.
[8] Alberto Melucci, *Nomads of the Present: Social Movements and Individual Needs in Contemporary Society* (Radius, Hutchinson, London, 1989).
[9] Alain Touraine, *The Post-Industrial Society* (Random House, New York, 1971).
[10] Reich, *The Work of Nations*, p. 178.
[11] Giddens calls these symbols 'disembedding mechanisms'. The key

characterisitic of modernity was what he calls 'time-space distantiation', in which social relations can be constructed with 'absent'
others. He defines globalization as a stretching of time–space
distantiation. See Anthony Giddens, *The Conditions of Modernity*
(Polity Press, Cambridge, 1990).

[12] This definition was developed by Radha Kumar. See Mary Kaldor
and Radha Kumar, 'New forms of conflict', in *Conflicts in Europe:
Towards a New Political Approach*, Helsinki Citizens' Assembly Publication Series 7, Prague, 1993.

[13] In his analysis of conflicts involving political Islam, Muhamed El
Said Said distinguishes between Islam based on missionary politics
and Islam based on identity politics. The Iranian revolution is an
example of the former, while Islamic movements in India are an
example of the latter. See 'Conflicts involving Islam', in Mary Kaldor
and Basker Vashee (eds), *Restructuring the Global Military Sector:
Volume I: New Wars* (Cassell / Pinter, London, 1997).

[14] I am indebted to Ivan Vejvoda for this point.

[15] The term is used by Katherine Verdery in 'Nationalism and national
sentiment in post-socialist Rumania', *Slavic Review*, Summer 1993.

[16] Ibid., p. 82. See also Robert M. Hayden, 'Constitutional nationalism in the formerly Yugoslav republics', *Slavic Review*, 51 (1992).

[17] This argument is also developed by Katherine Verdery. See, in particular, 'Ethnic relations, economies of shortage and the transition
in Eastern Europe', in C. M. Hann (ed.), *Socialism: Ideals, Ideology
and Local Practice* (Routledge, London, 1993).

[18] See, for example, Andrei Amalrik, *Will the Soviet Union Survive
Until 1984?* (Penguin Books, London, 1970), or Hélène Carrère
d'Encausse, *Decline of an Empire: The Soviet Socialist Republics in
Revolt* (Newsweek Books, New York, 1979).

[19] Teresa Rakowska-Harmstone, 'The dialectics of nationalism in the
USSR', *Problems of Communism*, XXIII, 1 (1974).

[20] In many cases, these titular nationalities were artificial. Tadjikistan,
for example, is an invented territorial unit. The Tadjik language is a
Persian dialect spoken in parts of Iran and Afghanistan which was
given a Cyrillic alphabet. The main Tadjik centres of civilization,
Samarkand and Bukhara, ended up outside the borders of Tadjikistan
in Uzbekistan.

[21] Victor Zaslavsky, 'Success and collapse: traditional Soviet nationality policy', in Ian Bremmer and Ray Taras (eds), *Nations and Politics
in Soviet Successor States* (Cambridge University Press, Cambridge,
1993).

[22] See, for example, Peter Lewis, 'From prebendalism to predation:
the political economy of decline in Nigeria', *Journal of Modern
African Studies*, 34, 1 (March 1996); Obi Igwara, 'Holy Nigerian

nationalisms and apocalyptic visions of the nation', *Nations and Nationalism*, 1, 3 (November 1995); Kisangani N. F. Ermizet, 'Zaire after Mobutu: a case of a humanitarian emergency', *WIDER Research for Action 32* (UNU/WIDER, Helsinki, 1997).

23 See Human Rights Watch, *Playing the Communal Card: Communal Violence and Human Rights* (New York, 1995).

24 Particularly fascinating in Greece is the way in which the civil war has been reinterpreted in recent years. Earlier, it was interpreted as an ideological conflict. Had it not been for the Anglo-American intervention and the pressure on Stalin and Tito to withdraw, it was argued, Greece would have been a socialist country. Now it is argued that the main aim of the communists was to create a united Macedonia including the Greek and Bulgarian parts. Hence, anti-Macedonian attitudes represent a way of distancing oneself from a past sympathy with communism.

25 For a description of this phenomenon in various places, see the Médecins Sans Frontières Report on World Crisis Intervention, *Life Death and Aid* (Routledge, London, 1993). In Liberia, Charles Taylor's National Patriotic Front of Liberia is described as marching on the capital: 'Constantly drunk or high on Marijuana, wearing wigs, wedding dresses or welder's goggles, they acted out the profound identity crisis in which their shattered world has led them', p. 56.

26 Rakiya Omaar and Alex de Waal, *Rwanda: Death, Despair and Defiance* (Africa Rights, September 1994), p. 35.

27 Šumit Ganguly, 'Explaining the Kashmir insurgency: political mobilisation and institutional decay', *International Security*, 21, 2 (Fall 1996).

28 Radha Kumar, 'Nationalism, nationalities and civil society', in *Nationalism and European Integration: Civil Society Perspectives*, Helsinki Citizens' Assembly Publication Series 2, Prague, 1991.

29 See Oliver Roy, *The Failure of Political Islam* (Taurus, London, 1994); see also Ernest Gellner, *Postmodernism, Reason and Religion* (Routledge, London and New York, 1992).

30 A. D. Smith, *Nations and Nationalism in a Global Era* (Polity Press, Cambridge, 1996).

31 Kwame Anthony Appiah, 'Cosmopolitan patriots', *Critical Inquiry* (Spring 1997), 618.

32 See Robert D. Kaplan, 'The coming anarchy', *Atlantic Monthly* (February 1994).

Chapter 5   The Globalized War Economy

1 Jeffrey Herbst, 'Responding to state failure in Africa', *International Security*, 21, 3 (Winter 1996/7), 121–2.
2 Human Rights Watch, *Playing the Communal Card: Communal Violence and Human Rights* (New York, 1995).
3 David Keen, 'When war itself is privatized', *Times Literary Supplement* (December 1995).
4 For details on this story, see David Shearer, 'Private armies and military invention', *Adelphi Paper 316* (IISS, London, February 1998).
5 International Institute for Strategic Studies, *Military Balance 1996–7* (Brasseys, London, 1997), p. 237.
6 Quoted in Simkin, *Race to the Swift: Thoughts on Twenty First Century Warfare* (Brasseys, London, 1985), p. 311.
7 The great exception, widely quoted, was the British experience in Malaya. However, the revolutionary movement was quite limited, mainly consisting of the Chinese minority. Nevertheless, what is interesting is the way in which, in contrast to other counterinsurgency practices, the British copied revolutionary tactics by trying to win 'hearts and minds' through the promise of independence and using similar military tactics to the guerrillas. See ibid.
8 Human Rights Watch, *Playing the Communal Card*, p. 9.
9 Quoted in Irving Lewis Horowitz, *Taking Lives: Genocide and State Power*, 4th edition (Transaction Books, New Brunswick, 1997). According to Horowitz, genocide is a state activity and is contrasted with vigilantism which is carried out by private groups, e.g. the Ku Klux Klan.
10 For the earlier figures see Dan Smith, *The State of War and Peace Atlas* (Penguin Books, London, 1997). The figure for the 1990s is my own calculation; see Mary Kaldor, 'Introduction', in Mary Kaldor and Basker Vashee (eds), *Restructuring the Global Military Sector: Volume I: New Wars* (Cassell/Pinter, London, 1997).
11 UNHCR, *The State of the World's Refugees: In Search of Solutions* (Oxford University Press, Oxford, 1995).
12 These figures can be found in the regular *World Refugee Survey* published by the US Committee on Refugees, Washington, DC.
13 Myron Weiner, 'Bad neighbours, bad neighbourhoods: an inquiry into the causes of refugee flows', *International Security*, 21, 1 (Summer 1996).
14 Mark Duffield, 'The political economy of internal war: asset transfer, complex emergencies and international aid', in Joanna Macrae and Anthony Zwi (eds), *War and Hunger: Rethinking International Responses* (Zed Press, London, 1994).

[15] David Keen has described the way in which the famine in Southern Sudan was caused by cattle-raiding by Baggara militiamen in the North supported by the Sudanese government as a way of weakening the SPLA (Sudan People's Liberation Army) which operated from the South: 'For young Baggara men, particularly those severely hit by economic marginalisation and drought, raiding offered the prospect of increasing their meagre capital stock.' David Keen, 'A disaster for whom? Local interests and international donors during famine. Among the Dinka of Sudan', *Disasters* 15, 2, 155.

[16] 'Central Asia's narcotics industry', *Strategic Comments*, 3, 5 (June 1997); 'Colombia's escalating violence: crime, conflict and politics', *Strategic Comments*, 3, 4 (May 1997).

[17] Duffield, 'Political economy of internal war', p. 56.

[18] Keen, 'When war itself is privatized'.

[19] John Simpson, *In the Forests of the Night: Encounters in Peru with Terrorism, Drug-running and Military Oppression* (Arrow Books, London, 1994).

[20] Keen, 'When war itself is privatized'.

[21] A Norwegian psychologist describes a session with 'Ivan', a boy from Bosnia–Herzegovina:

> How can one talk to a nine year old child about the fact that his father shot his best friend?
> I asked him for his own explanation, and he looked me right in the eyes and said 'I think they have been drinking something that has been poisoning their brains.' But he suddenly added, 'But now they are all poisoned, so I'm sure it is in the drinking water, and we really have to find out how to clean the polluted water reservoirs.' When I asked him if children were as much poisoned as adults he shook his head and said 'No, not at all. They have smaller bodies, so they are less contaminated, and I have discovered that small children and babies who mostly drink milk, they are not poisoned at all.'
> I asked him if he had ever heard the word politics. He almost jumped and looked at me and said, 'Yes. That's the name of the poison.'

Quoted in Dan Smith, *State of War and Peace*, p. 31.

[22] Several writers refer to the predatory character of contemporary war economies. See Xavier Bougarel, *L'Anatomie d'un conflit* (Edition Découverts, Paris, 1995), whom I quote in chapter 3. See also R. T. Naylor, 'The insurgent economy: black market operations of guerrilla organizations', *Crime Law and Social Change*, 20 (1993), and Peter Lewis, 'From prebendalism to predation: the political economy of decline in Nigeria', *Journal of Modern African Studies*, 34, 1 (March 1996).

[23] Michael Cranna (ed.), *The True Cost of Conflict* (Saferworld, Earthscan, 1994).

[24] See Vesna Bojičić, Mary Kaldor and Ivan Vejvoda, 'Post-war reconstruction in the Balkans', *European Foreign Affairs Review*, 2, 3 (Autumn 1997).

[25] By the end of 1986, the USA had supplied some $3 billion worth of aid. Some was diverted by the CIA to Nicaragua and Angola; some was diverted by Pakistani military intelligence for its own use and for the black market; some was sold by political leaders; and some was diverted by the arms suppliers through inflated invoices and pilfered cargoes. According to Naylor: 'The result was that not only did international aid organizations have to scour the bazaars to buy back the diverted food, clothing, tents and medicine, but those Afghan rebel chiefs who actually did fight sometimes had to use the profits of the heroin traffic to buy weapons that had already been paid for by the US and Saudi Arabia', 'The insurgent economy', p. 19.

[26] Duffield, 'Political economy of internal war', p .57.

Chapter 6   Towards a Cosmopolitan Approach

[1] See Michael Walzer, *Just and Unjust Wars: A Moral Argument with Historical Illustrations* (Pelican Books, London, 1980).

[2] Hannah Arendt, *Reflections on Violence* (Harcourt, Brace and Company, London and New York, 1979), pp. 50–1.

[3] 'Perpetual Peace' (1795), in Hans Reiss (ed.), *Kant's Political Writings* (Cambridge University Press, Cambridge, 1992).

[4] 'The law of armed conflict had the purpose of restricting the uses of violence between states and, in the case of civil wars, between governments and rebels. Human rights law had (among other things) the purpose of averting and restricting the uses of violence by governments towards their subjects whether formally in rebellion or not; a field of conflict for which international law, by definition, brought no remedies.' Geoffrey Best, *War and Law Since 1945* (Oxford: Clarendon Press, 1994).

[5] On the references to humane or cosmopolitan law, see J. Pictet, 'International humanitarian law: a definition', in UNESCO, *International Dimensions of Humanitarian Law* (Marinus Nijhoff, Dordrecht, 1988).

[6] For good introductions to the literature, see Oliver Ramsbotham and Tom Woodhouse, *Humanitarian Intervention in Contemporary Conflict: A Reconceptualization* (Polity Press, Cambridge, 1996); Ian Forbes and Mark Hoffman, *Political Theory, International Relations and the Ethics of Intervention* (Macmillan, London, 1993).

7 Adam Roberts, 'Humanitarian action in war', *Adelphi Paper 305*, IISS (OUP, London, 1996).
8 See Radha Kumar, 'The troubled history of partition', *Foreign Affairs*, 76, 1 (January/February 1997).
9 David Bremmer, 'Local peace and the South African transition', *Peace Review*, 9, 2 (June 1997).
10 William Warfield, 'Moving from civil war to civil society', *Peace Review*, 9, 2 (June 1997).
11 Ed Garcia, 'Filipino zones of peace', *Peace Review*, 9, 2 (June 1997).
12 *Times Literary Supplement*, 21 February 1997.
13 Quoted in ibid., p. 30.
14 Alex de Waal, *Famine Crimes: Politics and the Disaster Relief Industry in Africa* (Africa Rights and the International African Institute, Indiana University Press, Bloomington and Indianapolis, 1997), p. 178. See also Mohamed Sahnoun, *Somalia: The Missed Opportunities* (US Institute for Peace, Washington, DC, 1994).
15 See, for example, William J. Durch (ed.), *The Evolution of UN Peacekeeping: Case Studies and Comparative Analysis* (St Martin's Press, New York, 1993); Ministry of Defence, *Wider Peacekeeping* (HMSO, London, 1995); Mats R. Berdal, 'Whither UN peacekeeping?', *Adelphi Paper 281* (IISS, London, 1993).
16 See, for example, John Mackinlay and Jarat Chopra, *A Draft Concept of Second Generation Multinational Operations* (The Thomas J. Watson Jr. Institute for International Studies, Providence, RI, 1993).
17 Charles Dobbie, 'A concept for post-Cold War peace-keeping', *Survival*, Autumn 1994.
18 'Torture, rape, pillage and even cannibalism by ECOMOG supported factions hurt ECOMOG's general political acceptance.' Herbert Howe, 'Lessons of Liberia: ECOMOG and regional peace-keeping', *International Security*, 21, 3 (Winter 1996/7), p. 163.
19 Quoted in Africa Rights, *Somalia and Operation Restore Hope: A Preliminary Assessment* (London, May 1993). p. 28.
20 Roberts, 'Humanitarian action', p. 51.
21 John Mackinlay, 'Improving multifunctional forces', *Survival*, Autumn 1994. In fact, Mackinlay is himself confused. He goes on to say: 'Where force is used, impartiality [here he means neutrality] may seem to have been lost, especially by the party concerned. If legitimacy is intact, however, the appearance of impartiality can be restored.' What is important here is legitimacy in the eyes of the local population. It may not be possible to restore neutrality, which he refers to as impartiality, since the warring parties are no respecters of rules. The point is to retain impartiality from the point of view of the victims.
22 Quoted in Dobbie, 'A concept', p. 137.

23 Ioan Lewis and James Mayall, 'Somalia', in James Mayall (ed.), *The New Interventionism 1991–4: United Nations Experience in Cambodia, Former Yugoslavia, and Somalia* (Cambridge University Press, Cambridge, 1996), p. 117.
24 There have been reports of human rights abuses by UN personnel in Cambodia, Bosnia–Herzegovina, Somalia and Mozambique. Abuses have included rape, killings and involvement in child prostitution in Mozambique. See, for example, Africa Rights, *Somalia: Human Rights Abuses by the UN Forces* (London, July 1993).
25 Mark Duffield, 'Relief in war zones: towards an analysis of the new aid paradigm', *Third World Quarterly*, 1997.
26 Alvaro de Soto and Graciana del Costillo, 'Obstacles to peace-building' *Foreign Policy*, 94 (Spring 1994).
27 Africa Rights, *Somalia and Operation Restore Hope*.
28 Mats Berdal, 'Disarmament and demobilization after civil wars', *Adelphi Paper 303*, IISS (OUP, London, 1996).
29 Alex de Waal, 'Contemporary warfare in Africa', in Mary Kaldor and Basker Vashee, (eds), *Restructuring the Global Military Sector: Volume I: New Wars* (Cassell/Pinter, London, 1997), p. 331.

Chapter 7   Governance, Legitimacy and Security

1 London, Verso, 1996.
2 Samuel P. Huntington, *The Clash of Civilizations and the Remaking of World Order* (Simon and Schuster, New York, 1996); also 'The clash of civilizations?', *Foreign Affairs*, Summer 1993.
3 The neo-medievalism thesis is usually accredited to Umberto Eco, *Travels in Hyperreality* (Picador, London, 1987). For a description, see Barry Smart, *Postmodernity* (Routledge, London, 1996). It should be distinguished from Bull's New Medievalism which referred to the idea of overlapping political sovereignties and is closer to the cosmopolitan governance approach. Hedley Bull, *The Anarchical Society: A Study of Order in World Politics* (Macmillan, London, 1977).
4 Robert D. Kaplan, 'The coming anarchy', *The Atlantic Monthly* (February 1994); and Robert D. Kaplan, *The Ends of the Earth: A Journey at the Dawn of the Twenty First Century* (Papermac, London, 1997).
5 According to Martin Van Creveld: 'Truth to say, what we are dealing with here is neither low-intensity conflict nor some bastard off-spring of war. Rather it is WARRE in the elemental Hobbesian sense of the word, by far the most important conflict of our time.' Van Creveld, *The Transformation of War* (Free Press, Macmillan, London, 1991), p. 22.

6 Mary Kaldor, 'New world order: war of the imagination', *Marxism To-day* (13 February 1991).
7 Huntington, *The Clash of Civilizations*, p. 321.
8 Kaplan, *The Ends of the Earth*, p. 6.
9 Ibid., p. 45.
10 Ibid., p. 329.
11 Ibid., p. 432.
12 Quoted in David Keen, 'Organized chaos: not the new world we ordered', *World Today*, January 1996.
13 Kaplan, *The Ends of the Earth*, p. 337.
14 Ibid., p. 436.
15 *On Humane Governance* (Polity Press, Cambridge, 1995).
16 David Beetham, 'Human rights as a model for cosmopolitan de- mocracy', in Daniele Archibugi and David Held (eds), *Reimagining Political Community: Studies in Cosmopolitan Democracy* (Polity Press, Cambridge, forthcoming).
17 See Daniele Archibugi and David Held (eds), *Cosmopolitan Democracy: An Agenda for a New World Order* (Polity Press, Cambridge, 1995).

Afterword

1 The Commission was initiated by the Swedish Prime Minister and was chaired by Richard Goldstone, the first chief prosecutor of the United Nations International Criminal Tribunals for the former Yugoslavia and Rwanda. See *The Kosovo Report* (Oxford University Press, 2000) and also *www.kosovocommission.org*
2 *Doctrine of the International Community* 22 April 1999, Hilton Ho- tel, Chicago, Illinois.
3 Noel Malcolm, *Kosovo: A Short History* (Macmillan, London, 1998).
4 Some 2,000 families were reconciled and some 20,000 people were released from house arrest. A 'Council of Reconciliation' was estab- lished which tracked down Albanian families (even those living abroad) and brought them together for a mass reconciliation; this event then spawned the Pan-national Movement for the Reconcili- ation of Blood Vendettas. See Andrew March and Rudra Sil, *The 'Republic of Kosova' (1989–1998) and the Resolution of Ethno- Separatist Conflict in the Post-Cold War Era: Implications of a Post-Westphalian View of Sovereignty?* (University of Pennsylvania, Philadelphia, forthcoming).
5 Quoted in Tim Judah, 'Kosovo's Road to War', *Survival* (Summer 1999), p. 12.
6 Maggie O'Kane, 'The Terrible Day when Frenki's Boys came Call- ing', *Guardian* (19 June 1999).

[7] The number of deaths is widely disputed. These figures represent the best estimate of the IICK based on the collation of a wide range of reports from NGOs and other sources. See Annex 1, 'Documention on Human Rights Violations', *The Kosovo Report*.

[8] Richard Caplan, 'International Diplomacy and the Crisis in Kosovo', *International Affairs*, 74, 4 (October 1998), p. 752.

[9] See Gramoz Pashko, 'Kosovo: Facing Dramatic Economic Decline', in Thanos Veremis and Evangelos Kofos, *Kosovo: Avoiding another Balkan War* (ELIAMEP, University of Athens, 1998).

[10] *Observer* (18 July 1999).

[11] John Arquilla, 'The "Velvet" Revolution in Military Affairs', *World Policy Journal*, 14/4 (Winter 1997–8).

[12] See Ministry of Defence, *Lessons from the Crisis*, Cmnd 4724 (HMSO, London, 2000); House of Commons, Select Committee on Defence, Fourteenth Report, Session 1999–2000 (HMSO, London, 2000).

Index